John G. Kappas, Ph.D., founder and director of the Hypnosis Motivation Institute in Van Nuys, California, has more than 30 years' experience in the fields of hypnotherapy, sex therapy, and relationship counseling. He has written extensively on the subject of hypnotherapy and is recognized world-wide as an authority in the field.

Improve Your Sex Life through Self-Hypnosis

John G. Kappas, Ph.D.

Prentice-Hall, Inc.
Englewood Cliffs, New Jersey 07632

Library of Congress Cataloging in Publication Data

Kappas, John G.
Improve your sex life through self-hypnosis.

Includes index.
1. Sexual disorders—Treatment.   2. Autogenic training.
I. Title.
RC556.K34   1984   616.6'906512   83-27077
ISBN 0-13-453374-7
ISBN 0-13-453366-6 (A Reward book : pbk.)

This book is available at a special discount when ordered in bulk quantities. Contact Prentice-Hall, Inc., General Publishing Division, Special Sales, Englewood Cliffs, N.J. 07632.

5 6 7 8 9 10

ISBN 0-13-453374-7

ISBN 0-13-453366-6 {A REWARD BOOK : PBK.}

Editorial/production supervision by Peter Jordan
Manufacturing buyer: Pat Mahoney
Cover design by Hal Siegel

Prentice-Hall International, Inc., *London*
Prentice-Hall of Australia Pty. Limited, *Sydney*
Prentice-Hall Canada Inc., *Toronto*
Prentice-Hall of India Private Limited, *New Delhi*
Prentice-Hall of Japan, Inc., *Tokyo*
Prentice-Hall of Southeast Asia Pte. Ltd., *Singapore*
Whitehall Books Limited, *Wellington, New Zealand*
Editora Prentice-Hall do Brasil Ltda., *Rio de Janeiro*

Contents

Preface

Ever since Adam was introduced to Eve, sex has been one of the most potentially pleasurable of all human experiences. It is our most intimate method of sharing. It is recreation, procreation, and delightful fun. Yet there are times when everyone has a problem in bed. Sometimes we are just unable to put aside the cares of our busy workday. At other times the pressures are more subtle—subconscious memories that slowly build inside our heads until they dominate our relationships without our knowing why.

Improve Your Sex Life Through Self-Hypnosis teaches you the secrets of joyous sex. It explains your sexual personality, the reasons you are attracted to the opposite sex, and why you occasionally have difficulty with this most pleasant of all human experiences.

The book discusses sexual problems that can arise through no fault of your own. It then goes on to explain the techniques of self-hypnosis. Through this tool of both the conscious and subconscious mind, you will learn to focus your thoughts, ending the power of the past to dominate the pleasure of the present. You will be able to end or avoid such concerns as premature orgasm for a man and failure to climax for a woman. You will learn to increase the intensity of your sexual relations and achieve a more complete experience than you ever thought possible. You will also gain an understanding of yourself and your past as it may have been affecting your relationships.

For those who have had no difficulty with their sex lives, there is a section on increasing enjoyment. This section tells how to make a good experience an even greater one through the use of self-hypnosis. You will also be able to use the information concerning your sexual personality to select the perfect mate and maintain the best possible relationship with your lover or spouse.

The information in this book has been compiled through my experiences with thousands of couples from all walks of life. It has helped them overcome problems or simply increase their pleasures. I am confident that when you have finished reading this book, you will share their enthusiasm for the ways in which self-hypnosis can improve your sex life.

Improve your sex life through self-hypnosis

1

It has been said that sex is the most fun two people can have without bursting out laughing. Sex is a delightful, natural part of a growing relationship. The sex act not only is the means for procreation, it is also a thoroughly enjoyable way to spend time with a spouse or lover. But if sex is so basic to the human condition, why do so many people have problems with their sexual relationships? And why do some people feel that there is something lacking when they do enjoy sex?

The purpose of this book is to help you understand yourself as a sexual being and to learn to improve your sexual relations with your partner. It is a book that will show you the many subconscious factors that affect our relationships and the ways in which you, like so many others, can overcome those problems. If your sex life is already enjoyable but you think it could be better, this book will show you ways to increase your pleasure.

Why Are There Problems with Sex?

The sex act is not just a physical activity as many people think. It is a combination of mind, body, emotions, and previous conditioning.

2

The first phase of sex is in the mind. There must be a desire for the sex act, which frequently comes from fantasy. This occurs between casual lovers, individuals who have been dating for many months but have not yet had sex, and couples who wait until marriage for the first sex act. No matter when sex occurs in a relationship, it always starts with fantasy.

> "The first time I saw Jane, I noticed her large breasts and tight waist. All I could think about was what it might be like to fondle her," said Byron, discussing his fantasy about the woman who eventually became his lover. "We had several dates before we went to bed, but each time I mentally undressed her. When we finally became lovers, I could hardly wait to touch her, to see if she felt like I imagined she would."

> "I have this big waterbed," said Linda. "It takes up almost every inch of room in my apartment bedroom. When I'm thinking about getting serious with a guy, I always imagine what he would be like lying naked on top of the bed, his body moving with the water, as I go down on him."

The fantasies are as numerous as people. One woman thought about how her lover might look in a small country house she had always wanted. She pictured him by the front gate, playing with the children, to decide whether or not she was interested in him. Another liked to think of herself living in the Middle Ages, being carried off by a man on a large horse. There are rape fantasies, fantasies about sexual variations such as oral sex, and numerous others, all shared by both men and women.

Sometimes the fantasy is just anticipating the act to come. A couple may be driving from a nightclub to an apartment, the man thinking about how he will serve some wine, perhaps make something to eat, they will talk, listen to music, then drift off into the bedroom. However each person handles the fantasy, it is the essential preparation for sex.

Next comes the physical phase of the sexual relationship. There is touching of the body, kissing, perhaps undressing of each other. The body temperature rises, and there is increased awareness of the genital area. This continues until there is such intense focus that you advance to the third phase of intercourse and orgasm.

Finally, there is the fourth phase which I call the pre-fantasy phase. You and your lover are spent, the sexual arousal over. You may separate, either by one partner leaving the bed or by going to sleep, or you may talk and fondle each other for awhile. However, in order to begin the process again, there must be a return to the fantasy stage, preparing for the second orgasm.

Problems can arise at any stage in the first three phases of intercourse. They also can arise in certain relationships and not others, all because of preconditioning. Take the case of Herb, a stockbroker who was having trouble in his relationship with his wife, Beverly.

My parents came from one of those very strict, oddball religious backgrounds where you only have sex to make children, and you never enjoy the act without feeling guilty. I was always told that sex before marriage was wrong. Sex for pleasure, even in marriage, was wrong. Sex was for having babies and nothing else. Even thinking about sex was dirty.

I remember one time when a friend of mine and I found an old copy of *Playboy* in the trash while walking behind some houses on our way home from school. I took it home with me, and my mother caught me looking at it. She almost killed me, calling me sinful and dirty-minded. She went to church and told the minister so he could pray for my soul.

Finally I went away to college and began dating. At first I was a little inhibited because I kept feeling guilty about being aroused all the time. Finally I talked with some of the other guys who admitted they felt the same way around girls. I decided to stop trying to live the way my parents did and let whatever happened happen. That's when I met Sue and lost my virginity.

Sue was a really nice girl in my English class. We studied together at the library, went on dates a few times, and finally one thing led to another when we were parked in a car on a hill overlooking the campus. I felt absolutely wonderful. I had never enjoyed something so much in my life, and I realized that sex was fun, not something dirty.

There were other girls after Sue. I wasn't promiscuous and I never went the singles bar scene. But when I got serious about a girl, sex became a natural part of the relationship.

Finally I met Beverly and I knew she was the one for me. We got married just before my thirtieth birthday and my parents were thrilled. They knew Beverly only had a few years left to have children, and they were certain we would have a family immediately.

Beverly and I are both career-oriented and a family was the last thought we had. Neither one of us was ready to be a parent and we both knew we wanted to enjoy our relationship together first. If we decided to have a family when it was biologically too late, we could always adopt.

Things were great for a couple of months, and then I began having trouble. I would be horny and really want Beverly, yet lose my erection when I started to enter her. Sometimes I even had trouble sustaining an erection during foreplay. I got disgusted with myself and wondered if there was something wrong with my manhood. I was afraid to tell Bev what I was thinking and finally started looking for ways to avoid sex. I'd work a lot of overtime so I could claim that I was exhausted. Or I'd pick a fight with Bev so she would get mad and not want me that night.

I didn't face how serious the problem had become until Beverly told me she wanted to give me a divorce. She assumed that the reason our sex life had deteriorated so badly was because there was someone else in my life. She loved me too much to let me live a lie. If I wanted someone else, she would give me up. That's when I knew I had to have help, Dr. Kappas.

I love Beverly more than anyone or anything I've ever known. She's all I could ever want from anyone. Yet I just can't seem to perform. What's wrong with me?

The reality for Herb was that his mind was working against him. He had been subconsciously programmed by his early upbringing to think that sex was dirty. He felt guilty about enjoying relations with his wife when there was no intention of having children with her. The actions he and Beverly were taking were perfectly normal and there was nothing wrong with their decision to concentrate on their careers for a while. There was also nothing wrong with the possibility that they would choose never to have children. But Herb's upbringing had been so ingrained in his mind that when he met the special woman for his life, he could no longer sexually perform. His subconscious mind was punishing him for being "naughty" in the manner his parents viewed his actions.

Herb's background may be far different from your own. However, within each of us there is often a past experience, long forgotten, which affects our actions for many years to come. And nowhere is this more evident than in sex, where our feelings of humiliation and emotional pain can be the greatest.

The ways in which the problems manifest themselves will vary with the person. Some men may suffer from impotence or premature ejaculation. Women may find that sex is painful or that they can never seem to have an orgasm. Or the reverse might be true, both men and women being unable to get enough sex with their partner because their needs are from suppressed feelings.

> "I'm not cheap, Dr. Kappas. I'm not a whore and I have definite standards in men," said Candace, a bookkeeper for a small manufacturing plant. "But I can't stop having sex with the men I date. I expect them to take me to bed and I'm quite a willing partner. Sometimes I feel terrible if we only have sex once during the night, yet I don't really love any of the men. I'm not even certain I know what love means."

Candace came from a family where her father believed that showing emotion was a sign of weakness.

> I don't remember his ever holding me on his lap or putting his arm around me when we would go someplace together. I remember that when I first learned to ride a two-wheeler, I kept falling down and getting up all day as I tried to gain my balance. I never cried or complained. Falling was part of learning and I just accepted that—unless my father was around. Then I would deliberately cry if I fell, hoping he would pick me up and kiss away my tears. But he never did.
>
> I tried to get good grades in school because my father said that was important. I did, too, proudly showing my report cards. On those rare occasions I got all high marks, he just told me he expected to see it continue. If I let one grade slip, he would scold me without ever saying anything good about the other grades. I never could seem to win his approval.

Again, the pattern was typical. Candace desperately wanted her father's approval but could never get it. Subconsciously she decided that maybe she was no good as a person. When she went on dates, she was willing to give the men what they wanted because it was a way of gaining their approval. Frequent sex reassured her that she was a good person. She developed what others saw as an insatiable sex drive which kept her from having an intense relationship with any one man. Yet it was not sex that she wanted but her father's affection, a fact buried inside her subconscious.

Men can be the same way. Their insecurity about their own manhood can lead to the endless conquests or extreme sex within a marital relationship. Such men may crave sex several times a day, an amount that is excessive because it puts an unrealistic strain on a relationship.

Why Self-Hypnosis Corrects Sex Problems

Self-hypnosis is one of the most natural mental states. It is a basic tool of the human mind which we have called upon probably since humans first walked the face of the earth. It is a means of concentrating our attention in a way that enables us to achieve whatever ends we desire, including coming to grips with past negative influences in our lives.

For example, have you ever left your office with a problem on your mind? There is an important meeting being planned and you know you must think about your role in it. As you drive along the freeway, a route you have taken every day for many months, you begin thinking about the problem.

Suddenly a large truck cuts in front of you, forcing you to both brake and check the cars around you in case evasive action is necessary. A few moments later, you change lanes, accelerating smoothly into the traffic. A tailgater pulls up behind you and you turn on your lights for a moment so that it looks like you are braking, forcing the tailgater to pull back to a safer distance. All the time that you are making these important decisions, your mind is focused on the problem at the office.

Time passes and you realize that this stretch of freeway is not familiar. You have missed your exit, perhaps going several miles out of your way. Your mind has been absorbed with the problem at the office, yet your driving has been flawless. You never endangered anyone around you. This ability to concentrate on one subject so intensely that you missed your exit, yet never lost control of the car, is a form of self-hypnosis.

Sometimes an extreme case of self-hypnosis makes the news. A mother hears a crash and screams. Her teenage son was working on his car when the jack slipped and he is pinned underneath. She races to the car and lifts one end, freeing him to crawl out. The woman, who weighs perhaps one hundred pounds fully clothed, lifted a far greater weight than seems possible. Again, she was under a state of self-hypnosis which enabled her to focus all the strength of the human body (approximately six to nine times greater than the strength we normally use) on the task that needed to be done—saving her child.

As another example, you have just had an argument with someone close to you before you begin walking down a crowded street. In your mind, you are thinking only of the fight, replaying the conversation mentally. All your attention is focused on what was said, what should have been said, and perhaps what will have to be said to restore the relationship to the way it was. You are in self-hypnosis at that moment. Your subconscious mind is going over and over past programming and your subconscious mind is on the fight.

Another example of this is if someone stops you and asks, "Didn't you hear me when I yelled hello to you?" "You walked by me like I wasn't even there." "I called your name a dozen times. How come you never responded?" And similar comments you have heard at times will be made. Once again, you were in a state of self-hypnosis.

Self-hypnosis is a potent tool for helping you with your sex life. First, after you have an understanding of your own sexuality, it can enable you to recall the past conditioning which has led to current sexual problems. Then, with this understanding, it is a simple matter to reprogram your subconscious mind so that you can truly enjoy this most delightful of all human activities.

Self-hypnosis can also enable you to improve your sexual relationships. You can learn to shift your sensate focus to have a deeper, more intense orgasm than you have ever experienced before. If you are one of the many women who climax rather than experience orgasms, you will be able to enjoy your sexual experience all the more. In some instances, you may be able to move from climax to the rolling pleasure of orgasm.

Women who have problems with tightness will be able to relax and enjoy penetration. Men who cannot have an orgasm after penetration without taking so long that the woman becomes numb will learn to better focus their feelings so that orgasm is more pleasurable for both.

But before we explore the field of self-hypnosis and the new sexual enjoyment you will be able to experience, let us first look at the nature of human sexuality. Who you are, what you feel, and the way you approach any deep relationship are products of your past that make you unique. By understanding what causes you to think and feel the way you do and what can cause your partner to view life in quite a different manner, you will be better equipped to improve your sexual and personal relationships.

Understanding sexuality: what turns you on

2

Have you and a friend ever stood in a crowded shopping mall or on a busy street corner, watching the passing parade of people? Suddenly you notice a particularly attractive man or woman and comment on this to your friend. Chances are your friend will agree, describing the handsomeness or beauty in a way that makes you realize you are not looking at the same person. The individual your friend finds so attractive has no appeal for you at all.

Each of us has certain sexual turn-ons which first attract us to another person. One man might like a woman with a big bust and carefully teased hair. Another man might find beauty in the small woman with narrow hips and tiny chest. Yet a third might notice legs first, not really caring about the rest of her appearance if the legs are attractive.

The same is true for women. One woman might see a man's face as his most important feature while another tends to notice his rear end before looking at the rest of his body.

There are also cultural attractions based on the way we were raised to think about the opposite sex. There was a time when women were considered the passive partner. Sex was part of a relationship which the male controlled. It was used for his gratification and for procreation. However, the advent of the birth control pill resulted in a new freedom for women. They felt they could take more control in a sexual relationship, becoming the aggressor if they so chose. It was a natural evolution and one which has delighted some men. Yet for others, the aggressive female is so contrary to the behavior they were taught to seek as children that her actions can be a sexual turn-off.

To fully understand your sex drives and the reasons problems can occur with any relationship, we must look at both sexuality and suggestibility, two different aspects of human behavior. Taken together, they affect all of our relationships and form a key which can help unlock the most enjoyable sexual experiences of which we are all capable.

Sexuality

This book is the result of a revolution in sexual understanding. We have learned that sexual relations are an enjoyable and natural aspect of human interaction. Improved methods of birth control allow greater sexual freedom, and better understanding of sex encourages couples to enjoy a variety of sexual activities with each other. No longer do we feel that variations from the basic missionary position are somehow wrong. We now understand that anything two consenting adults enjoy doing with each other which is not painful for either one is perfectly all right. We have been freed from the foolish myths and needless constraints of the past where right and wrong in sex were rigidly and arbitrarily defined.

Personal sexual expression is now understood to be almost as varied as fingerprints. Rather than trying to fit an individual's natural sexual personality into a special mold, most people today recognize that understanding their own sexual being can lead to greater happiness. More important is that such understanding can help you achieve far greater sexual enjoyment with another person than you have ever known.

This change in our sexual understanding, though positive, has also led to problems. A man who subconsciously feels that a woman is acting properly when she takes a passive role may become impotent when faced with an aggressive woman. Yet that same man may be greatly drawn to the woman, have many erotic fantasies about her, and be delighted that she wants a relationship with him. He does not realize that her behavior, quite proper for her natural sexuality, is bringing to the surface long-suppressed concerns which prevent him from functioning.

The reverse situation can also be true. Some women have been raised with an image of what a proper woman both feels and does with a man. She may try to fit this image, again quite different from her natural sexuality, and discover that she is unable to achieve orgasm. She truly wants the man who is making love with her but, again, there is subconscious repression.

Later in this book, you will learn to use self-hypnosis to counter this subconscious programming. But first, it is important to understand why you feel and behave the way you do in your relationships.

Types of Sexuality

In my many years of doing therapy, I have discovered that there are actually two major types of individuals. I have named them the physical sexual and the emotional sexual. These variations began to appear in the 1930's and 1940's because of changes in our society.

There is a saying that opposites attract, and this is true with human sexuality. However, for many years, our society did not allow for the natural selection of marriage partners. Some Americans came from ethnic and cultural backgrounds where marriages were prearranged. Jewish parents might use a marriage broker to select the mate for their child. Oriental couples might plan the union of their children while their sons and daughters were quite young. Wealthy society members often demanded that their children marry according to whatever merger might be best both socially and for the business the son would be entering. And in small communities, where transportation was limited and travel almost nonexistent, the small population base restricted free choice.

Eventually, our country developed in different ways. Transportation improved and young people no longer felt restricted to their immediate community. The assimilation of different cultures resulted in their selecting mates according to personal attraction and not according to the desires of their families. Interracial and interreligious marriages became common, again eliminating the old barriers.

With this natural selection process, opposites were drawn together routinely. This meant that children born into such families had very different parents. Behavior patterns that might please one parent would not necessarily gain the approval of the other. Even the way in which their parents spoke to them might have very different meanings. Thus most adults under the age of fifty have developed their natural sexuality as a result of parents who were opposites to each other.

Most people have both physical and emotional sexual tendencies although they are more comfortable with one extreme than the other. Individuals who are classed as physical sexuals project their sexuality outward. These are people who may wear clothing which calls attention to their bodies, such as open shirts and low-cut blouses. They like to touch and be touched, often moving closer to the person with whom they are sitting as they talk. They are comfortable with their physical bodies and will try to lead active sex lives, since sex, in itself, can provide a reassuring sense that they are wanted.

The emotional sexual is not so comfortable with the physical body, though he or she may have a very active, enjoyable sex life. This is the person who may wear high-necked clothing and subdued colors which do not call attention to him or her when in public. The emotional sexual likes to keep a certain distance when talking and may react with a blush or other sign of embarrassment in the midst of talk about sex.

In order to illustrate the differences between physical and emotional sexuality, I will be discussing extremes. Most people will have some of each trait, though one form of sexuality will be dominant. However, it is easiest to understand yourself and your sex partner if you know the extremes. Later in this book, you will take a test that will give you your specific sexuality. Women are more likely to be emotional sexuals and men more likely to be physical sexuals, though often the ratio for each person is in the nature of sixty percent of one to forty percent of the other.

Almost everyone has two important people in his or her life from the moment of birth. Usually these are the parents, especially during the early, formative years. Even with the high divorce rate, most children are likely to have a father and mother present for the first few years of life.

In single parent homes, there are still likely to be two important individuals. One may be the mother and the other an uncle, close friend of the mother, or some other relative, male or female.

The two people in the newborn's and growing child's life can be described as the primary caretaker and the secondary caretaker. One person, usually the mother, is most likely to appear when there are needs. A baby cries when hungry and the mother comes with breast or bottle. A baby cries when wet and the mother is usually the one who comes to change the diaper. A baby cries when hurt and the mother is most often the comforter. The baby quickly learns that survival depends upon relating to and pleasing the mother or other primary caretaker.

As the child grows, the secondary caretaker is viewed as someone who gives mother pleasure. She is happy with this person and, in the case of a husband or boyfriend, gives special attention to his needs. Since the child needs the mother's approval for both physical survival and personal happiness, he or she realizes that by imitating the actions of the person the mother seems to like most, the child will get approval. Thus we learn our sexuality from our fathers or whatever other person has taken the secondary caretaker role in our lives.

Naturally, parents who reverse traditional roles, having the father stay home to take care of the child while the mother works, will have the same situation prevail in reverse. The father becomes the primary caretaker and the child imitates the mother's sexuality in order to gain the father's approval. And when parents evenly divide the child-rearing chores, such as couples who each work a half day so that together they have one salary and equal time at home, the child has a combination of the two.

The physical sexual individual is one who places his or her body in a relationship in order to protect the emotions contained within. The physical sexual woman will often wear clothing meant to show off her body, such as low-cut blouses or blouses which are partially unbuttoned. She is very concerned with her dress and make-up because she is constantly aware of how others might be observing her. Maintaining her appearance is extremely important to her.

The physical sexual male is equally concerned with appearance. He will dress in fashions which show off his body. Depending upon current styles, he might have an open shirt, perhaps with gold chains around his neck, or he might wear a net-type top which barely covers his chest. He is the macho individual who avoids expressing concern about intellectual pursuits and is more interested in the physical.

The physical sexual man is extremely attentive to a woman. He will hold the door for her, light her cigarette, help her with her coat and chair, and otherwise be extremely courteous. He sees himself as the dominant person within any relationship and enjoys taking care of the woman during the courting period.

The physical female is often somewhat vain, desiring the men she dates to reinforce her sense of femininity. She is comfortable with the roles of wife and mother, and can become extremely jealous of other women during a love affair.

Both males and females enjoy sex with great frequency. They are easily hurt when a partner is not as interested as they are. The physical female may increase her efforts to please the man in order to regain his sexual interest in her. The physical male may do likewise, but he is also apt to seek a career in which he can work with his hands. He finds the physical activity an outlet for his intense sexual desires during those periods of the day when he cannot pursue them.

Because of the ease with which physical sexual men and women can be hurt by what they may perceive as rejection, they are actually controlled by their mates. They are anxious to please in order to be rewarded with sex. Thus they may demean themselves in an ongoing relationship to avoid the possibility of rejection.

Typical of this type of physical sexual male is the Casper Milquetoast who appears to be henpecked. He will cook, clean, take out the trash, and generally leap to do any whim his wife might have. To outsiders, the man seems to be henpecked. He appears to lack personal drive or even a sense of self-worth. Yet the reality is that he is doing all these things because he knows that by doing them, he will be rewarded in bed. As long as the sex is as frequent as he desires, he will do anything to avoid rejection.

Physical sexual males may have sex more times in an evening than the emotional male, whom I will describe shortly. However, this is not because he is some super stud capable of great activity. Instead, he does not release all of his semen when he has an orgasm. He retains a portion, so one or more additional orgasms are needed for full release. His opposite, the emotional sexual, releases all his semen when he climaxes, so it will naturally take him longer to become aroused again.

The physical sexual male has a strong need to dominate the female during the sex act. He likes to be on top during intercourse and does not particularly enjoy such sexual variations as oral sex. He will go to extremes to satisfy his partner, telling himself that he is trying to please her. In reality, he is enjoying the prolonging of the relationship and pleasing himself. However, he is more likely to be a long-term, faithful partner who tries to make a relationship work when there are problems than is the emotional sexual male.

The physical sexual female is extremely sensitive to criticism from her partner. She often will attack when hurt, remembering slights and throwing them back at her boy friend or spouse weeks, months, and even years later. She retains the resentment she feels and will throw it back at her spouse with such frequency that problems with the relationship can arise.

Once an argument is over, the physical sexual woman will want to make up right away, often by having sex. She sees the sex act as an acceptance of her emotionally and will only be hurt again if her partner fails to respond to her sexual desires at that time. Unfortunately, she is quite likely to be married to an emotional sexual male who has the tendency to withdraw following an argument.

The physical female uses her physical feelings to understand those around her, often being extremely intuitive. She takes the word of others literally, though she tends to infer ideas when she speaks.

Children and family are important to both the physical sexual male and female. The male has a relatively easy time relating to the children a woman may have from a previous marriage. Both enjoy sharing hobbies and activities.

The physical sexual male likes team sports, both as a player and as an active participant. He enjoys the company of other men and his conversation often will range from sex to sports and back to sex again.

Physical sexual men and women have the greatest problems with others when the relationship breaks up. Frequently, the partner was placed on a pedestal and he or she cannot understand why the reality was not what was expected. The hurt continues for many years and the person may not stop loving the spouse long after the break-up or divorce. The pain is both greater and lasts longer than occurs with the emotional sexual.

THE EMOTIONAL SEXUAL INDIVIDUAL

The emotional sexual man or woman is the opposite of the physical sexual. Where one is flashy, the other is subdued. The physical sexual might have clothing designed to show off the body while the emotional sexual wears clothes which are far more subtle. The physical sexual delights in driving a sports car while the emotional sexual prefers to own a more practical car.

The emotional sexual individual is more likely to be successful on the job than the physical sexual man or woman. This is because there is less preoccupation with sex and thus an easier time attending to the detailed work of management. Thus you will often find that physical sexuals are excellent in aggressive fields such as sales. However, the emotional sexuals will be better able to handle management tasks requiring close attention to detail. The physical sexual enjoys the flash; the emotional likes the behind-the-scenes work which may result in the real power within an organization.

The emotional sexual female has difficulty expressing herself. She holds back her true feelings, which usually are far greater than will be visible on the surface.

The emotional sexual female is as devoted to work and career as the physical sexual female may be devoted to home and family. She wants to be treated as an equal partner in a business or personal relationship, not as a subordinate. She will work effectively as an employee, but she will also seek to advance herself whenever the opportunity is available.

The emotional sexual male usually takes jobs that require him to work behind the scenes. He may seek or have great power within an organization, but he is not likely to be the person up front, attempting to greet the public.

The emotional sexual female has many woman friends, unlike the physical female who sees all other women as a personal threat. She will also take an interest in their appearance because she feels that her looks are somehow inferior to those of others. She admires their looks rather than trying to compete because she senses that she cannot compete, no matter how attractive others may find her.

The emotional male and female enjoy sports, though as participants, not observers. They are not the type to watch football games on a Sunday afternoon, for example. They would rather participate, usually in individual competition which may have a slight element of danger to it. The physical female might enjoy a softball team or bowling league while the emotional female may take up karate or skiing. Competitive emotional males and females may be found in track and field events in high school and college rather than in such group activities as basketball or soccer.

Sex is slow in coming for the emotional sexual female. First, there is a prolonged fantasy stage during which she is slow to mentally arouse herself. Then her body must be slowly warmed since she will have the tendency to feel physically cold. This warming comes from the slow touching of the sensitive areas of her body, areas which are usually far from the genitals. She is turned off by any immediate stroking of the genital area and responds best to touching of the neck, ears, abdomen, and other areas.

Once orgasm is achieved, the emotional sexual female wants to place some distance from her sex partner. She usually climaxes rather than has orgasms and then wants to do other things. She is not one to desire the lingering touch expected by the physical female after the sex act is completed.

The emotional female has a definite sexual cycle which varies from woman to woman. Typically, I have found that it will range from every three days to as long as once a month. It is at the high point of this cycle that she is most sexually responsive and has the greatest desire. The male also has such a cycle, though both can have sex more frequently.

Sex must be more spontaneous for the emotional female than for the physical female. A man can talk about having sex with a physical female and the anticipation, even if it is for an event which cannot take place for several hours, begins to arouse her. When a man talks about sex with the emotional female, such as suggesting that they should go to bed the moment he comes home from work, she is gradually turned off. She may resent the suggestion, even though a more spontaneous loving occurring after they are together would be welcome. As time passes, the more she thinks about the suggestion, the more her resentment builds. She may deliberately develop a headache or become involved with activities which prevent her from making the planned meeting.

It is important to understand that the emotional sexual female is not frigid and does not have a sex problem. She can have an orgasm and may thoroughly enjoy her sexual relations. She simply moves more slowly than her physical female counterpart and needs to be aroused somewhat differently. Because she tends to be drawn to the physical male who is ready to hop into bed with the slightest arousal, she may prove frustrating to a man who does not try to understand her needs. She may have difficulty talking about what will help her become aroused and have an enjoyable sexual experience, choosing to fake orgasm and endure his demands. However, when there is good communication and mutual understanding, she does have an enjoyable sex life.

Both the emotional sexual man and woman have a fairly frequent sex life during the early stages of a relationship. This is almost as intense as the drive of their physical sexual counterparts, though the drive fades over time in the relationship while it grows for the physical male and female.

The emotional male gradually comes to withdraw. He sees no sense in constantly telling a woman that she is attractive or what he is feeling for her. He assumes that she understands that when he voices no complaint, he is being approving. Unfortunately, he is usually married to a physical female who needs constant verbal attention to feel comfortable about herself.

There is a definite pattern to the life of the emotional male. He gradually puts the energy he put into sex during the early stages of the relationship into other activities, such as clubs, hobbies, or something similar. Sex is simply not all that important to him, though even his desires may fall into a particular pattern. There may be a certain time of day when he wants sex and desires a partner to be available for him, regardless of his wife's situation.

The result of all this is that the emotional sexual male is more likely to take a mistress than the physical sexual male. He likes the convenience of what amounts to sex on demand, the lack of other involvements on the woman's part, and the chance to fit her into his schedule. Typical is the business executive or politician who must often work late into the evening. His wife has children to handle, the house to maintain, and perhaps a job. He may be able to take an hour off sometime after five before returning to the rest of his work, but this occurs when his wife is busiest with the children. The mistress provides an exciting alternative who will meet his schedule because that is both her choice and the result of her relative freedom. She does not have the responsibilities that come with marriage and thus can be available on demand.

The emotional sexual male feels responsible for both his wife and mistress, though his feelings for each are quite different. He will go to great lengths to keep his wife from knowing about the mistress, though he often fantasizes about having them meet and get along with each other. Such fantasies are strongest on family holidays, such as Christmas, when he must be with his wife and children, yet wants to take care of his mistress on such a special day.

The emotional sexual may criticize other women in front of his wife, including his mistress if she knows the woman. He tries to make it clear that he is not attracted to another woman, even though he is seeing her regularly.

The wife becomes an obligation to the emotional male. Typically, I hear such comments as: "She is a good woman and a wonderful mother, but I just don't love her." He does not want a divorce and would rather drop his mistress than yield to her demands that he choose between the wife he does not love and the mistress he claims he does love. When a divorce occurs, it is usually initiated by the wife. Yet, even then, the man will probably not marry his mistress, choosing some other woman instead.

An emotional sexual male does not have to have a wife to cheat. Such a man may choose to live with a woman or have what amounts to a steady girl friend/sex partner, yet still have a second woman on the side. The second woman provides the excitement he may feel is missing in his current relationship.

Sex needs to be spontaneous for the emotional sexual male. He does not like the slow seduction of wining and dining the woman in order to lead up to the sex act.

Once sexual relations have begun, the emotional sexual male does not want to be distracted by talk. He enjoys stimulating the woman and watching what she does. He is happy being a passive partner, participating in oral sex and/or having her on top during intercourse. He may have difficulty keeping his mind on sex and thus will want everything she does to lead towards orgasm, with nothing distracting him from what they are doing.

The emotional sexual male has trouble dating while in high school. He may have many girls who are friends but he has difficulty when it comes to dating them. Thus he may marry his high school sweetheart, partially because he cares about her and partially because he is comfortable. He does not have to go through the courtship phase which he finds most difficult. Since this is usually a physical sexual female, she will enjoy his attention. She may also feel challenged to be aggressive towards him when he seems to pull away, thus helping to sustain the relationship.

Once married, the emotional sexual male does not want children and resents pregnancy. He is concerned with his career and other activities and is uncomfortable with the idea of a family which his wife will want. However, his drive for work will lead him to a level of success where he finally attains the self-confidence he was lacking in the high school years. Now he is ready to take an interest in other women, usually those who work where he does. He decides that his wife has not kept up with his interests and turns toward the women around him for extramarital affairs.

The main reason the emotional sexual woman does not behave similarly is because she is probably married to a physical sexual male. Her reduced sex drive relative to his drive will cause him to be increasingly attentive to her, hoping for sex as a reward. Sometimes this reward comes willingly if she is aroused. Other times she may fake orgasms or simply put him off, which only serves to increase his attentiveness. Although she may not feel satisfied emotionally or physically, she is in a situation of control which is pleasurable enough to continue the relationship.

Testing for Emotional and Physical Sexuality

Before we go any further, it is important for you to understand your personal sexuality. The following tests are meant to help you analyze the degree of emotional and physical sexuality which is natural for you. You may also use these tests to analyze your current sex partner, to better understand your similarities and differences.

Although these tests are quite simple, they have proven to be extremely accurate for the vast majority of my patients. Thus, I am quite confident that they will help you as we progress with learning how to improve your sex life through self-hypnosis.

Always keep in mind that the results are neither good nor bad. It is not better to have more of one type of sexuality than another. Both physical sexuality and emotional sexuality are quite natural and people at both extremes are able to enjoy active, fulfilling sex lives. However, without the knowledge of your sexuality, you will not be able to understand the differences in feelings, desires, and other phases of your relationship with your sex partner.

FEMALE SEXUALITY QUESTIONNAIRE #1

1. Answer *only one* (a, b, or c). You should answer *yes* if your parent(s) had one or more of the following traits.
   a. If you were raised by both parents (up to age fifteen or sixteen), was your father more possessive of you, or more outward and demonstrative in showing affection to you, than your mother?
   b. If you were raised by your father only, was he outward and demonstrative in showing affection for you?
   c. If you were raised by your mother only, was she outward and demonstrative in showing affection for you?
2. Does *b* more closely describe what you usually feel at the culmination of the sex act than *a*?
   a. A sudden end to all pleasurable feeling (stimulation may turn to an irritation or ticklish frustration) and a feeling of wanting to back off and stop sex momentarily or completely.
   b. A physical and emotional release with contractions, spasmodic shivering, body warmth, moisture, and capacity for multiple releases.
3. If your partner breaks off a relationship that you do not want to end, do you find that all your energies and thoughts keep drifting back to him and that you are unable to concentrate on anything else?
4. Do you enjoy being touched and caressed by your partner immediately after the sex act?
5. Are you more jealous and/or possessive of your sex partner than he is of you?
6. Do you often desire repeated intercourse when having sex with your partner?
7. Would you like your partner to be more sexually aggressive and creative than he is?

8. Does it disturb you if your sex partner's drive diminishes after the newness of the relationship wears off?

9. During the sex act, does it stimulate you to verbally express the different physical and emotional feelings you are experiencing?

10. If you feel that you have been unfairly criticized or rejected, are you capable of expressing extreme anger, tantrums, or vindictiveness?

11. Is the man in your life your number one priority?

12. Do you enjoy buying gifts for your partner?

13. Do you feel that having sex after an argument is a good way to make up?

14. Do you feel that you have a greater capacity for love and deep emotional feelings than your partner?

15. Do you enjoy receiving attention and flattery from your partner in the presence of others?

16. If you suspected your partner of cheating, would you put the greatest blame on the woman for leading him astray?

17. Do you feel that you are better able to express intimate feelings and attitudes than your partner?

18. Do you feel that you give more of yourself to your partner than he does to you?

19. Do you feel that one of the ultimate fulfillments of your womanhood is to have your own children?

20. Do you feel that you have a greater capacity for giving and receiving sex than your partner?

FEMALE SEXUALITY QUESTIONNAIRE #2

1. Answer *only one* (a, b, or c). You should answer *yes* if your parent(s) had any one or more of the traits listed.
   a. If you were raised by both parents (up to age fifteen or sixteen), was your father less possessive of you, or more passive and undemonstrative in showing affection for you, than your mother?
   b. If you were raised by your father only, was he undemonstrative, passive, cold, withdrawn, or overly strict?
   c. If you were raised by your mother only, was she undemonstrative, passive, cold, withdrawn, or overly strict?

2. Does *a* more closely describe what you usually feel at the culmination of the sex act than *b*?
   a. A sudden end to all pleasurable feelings (stimulation may turn to an irritation or ticklish frustration) and a feeling of wanting to back off and stop the sex act momentarily or completely.
   b. A physical and emotional release with contractions, spasmodic shivering, body warmth, moisture, and capacity for multiple releases.

3. During the sex act would you prefer to avoid verbally expressing the different physical and emotional feelings you are experiencing?

4. Do you find that as the newness of a relationship wears off your sex drive towards your partner diminishes?
5. Is the expectation of sex often greater than the actual physical act of sex?
6. Do you have the attitude that if you felt five minutes before the sex act as you do five minutes after, that you would never have sex?
7. During an argument, does your partner tend to throw back at you things you said or did in the past that hurt, angered, or rejected him?
8. When you are having sex with your partner, do you often fantasize about someone else or about another sex act?
9. Do you sometimes fake orgasm just to end the sex act?
10. Do you turn off sexually during heavy kissing or rough handling?
11. Do your hands and feet usually feel colder than the rest of your body?
12. Once you have reached climax or orgasm, do attempts by your partner to continue stimulation turn you off?
13. Are you constantly searching outside of your relationship for the romance you feel is missing in your relationship?
14. Does your partner desire sex more often than you do?
15. Do you turn off during sex if distracted by small talk or by something that you feel criticizes you?
16. Do you feel embarrassed or self-conscious if your partner touches you or handles you a great deal in public?
17. Would you avoid or refuse to have sex with your partner after an argument?
18. Do you make excuses to avoid sex with your partner at times?
19. Does it annoy you if you have to reassure your partner by giving him compliments or attention that he outwardly solicits from you?
20. Do you feel frustrated if you do not have some time for yourself away from your partner?

MALE SEXUALITY QUESTIONNAIRE #1

1. Answer *only one* (a, b, or c). You should answer *yes* it your parent(s) had any one or more of the traits listed.
   a. If you were raised by both parents (up to age fifteen or sixteen), was your father more possessive of you or more outward and demonstrative in showing affection for you, than your mother?
   b. If you were raised by your father only, was he outward and demonstrative in showing affection for you?
   c. If you were raised by your mother only, was she outward and demonstrative in showing affection for you?
2. Do you often desire repeated intercourse when having sex with your partner?
3. In a relationship, after a disagreement, do you usually make up first?

4. Are your more jealous and/or possessive of your partner than she is of you?

5. Do you feel that having sex after an argument is a good way to make up?

6. Do you like to show your partner attention by opening doors, helping her with her coat, pulling her chair out before she sits down, and the like?

7. Immediately following the sex act, do you like to touch and caress your partner?

8. If you feel you have been unfairly criticized or rejected by your partner, are you capable of expressing extreme anger, tantrums, or vindictiveness?

9. When you first meet someone of the opposite sex, are you first attracted to the area of her body from the waist down rather than from the waist up?

10. If you have been strongly rejected by your partner, do you feel actual physical discomfort or pain?

11. Is it important to you to share most of your social activities and hobbies with your partner?

12. If your partner breaks off a relationship that you do not want to end, do you find that all your energies and thoughts keep drifting back to her and you have difficulty concentrating on anything else?

13. Do you pacify your partner at times, even when you think she is wrong, in order to prevent her from turning off sexually?

14. Do you feel that you give more of yourself to your partner than she does to you?

15. Would you like your partner to be more sexually aggressive and creative than she is?

16. Do you enjoy receiving attention and flattery from your partner in the presence of others?

17. Is the woman in your life your number one priority?

18. If you suspected your partner of cheating, would you put the greatest degree of blame on the man for leading her astray?

19. Do you feel that you have a greater capacity for love and deep emotional feelings than your partner?

20. Does it disturb you if your partner's sex drive diminishes after the newness of the relationship wears off?

MALE SEXUALITY QUESTIONNAIRE #2

1. Answer *only one* (a, b, or c). You should answer *yes* if your parent(s) had any one or more of the traits listed.
   a. If you were raised by both parents (up to age fifteen or sixteen), was your father less possessive of you, or more passive and undemonstrative, in showing affection than your mother?
   b. If you were raised by your father only, was he undemonstrative, passive, cold, withdrawn, or overly strict?

    c. If you were raised by your mother only, was she undemonstrative, cold, withdrawn, passive, or overly strict?

2. Instead of complimenting your partner, do you usually take the attitude that as long as you do not complain, everything is okay?
3. Is the expectation of sex often greater than the actual physical act of sex?
4. Do you feel that it is an unnecessary act to open doors and light cigarettes for a woman, even though you may do it?
5. When you make up after a fight, do you still feel resentment and find it difficult to fully forgive?
6. Does your partner want sex more often than you do?
7. Do you dislike wining and dining a female in order to have sex (assuming that money is no object)?
8. Answer *only one* (a or b):
    a. If married, do you usually have or prefer to have a mistress or steady girl friend?
    b. If single, do you usually have one steady girl friend but date many other girls at the same time?
9. Would you avoid or refuse to have sex with your partner after an argument?
10. Would you rather avoid verbally expressing love, tenderness, and affection immediately following intercourse?
11. When you meet someone of the opposite sex, are you first attracted to the area of her body from the waist up rather than from the waist down?
12. Do you turn off during sex if distracted by small talk or something that you feel criticizes you?
13. Are you constantly searching outside of your relationship for the romance you feel is missing in your relationship?
14. Do you find that as the newness of a relationship wears off, your sex drive towards your partner diminishes?
15. Would you have a strong resentment against a female becoming pregnant by you except perhaps until you are well-established in a marriage and ready to have children?
16. Do you have the attitude that if you felt five minutes before the sex act as you feel five minutes after, that you would never have sex?
17. During the sex act, would you prefer to avoid verbally expressing the different physical and emotional feelings you are experiencing?
18. During an argument, does your partner tend to throw back at you things you said or did in the past that hurt, angered, or rejected her?
19. When you are having sex with your partner, do you often fantasize about someone else or about another sex act?
20. Does it annoy you if you have to reassure your partner by giving her compliments or attention that she outwardly solicits from you?

SCORING INSTRUCTIONS FOR SEXUALITY QUESTIONNAIRES

1. Count the number of *yes* answers on Questionnaire #1 and multiply by five.
2. Do the same for Questionnaire #2.
3. Add the two scores together to obtain the combined score.
4. Locate your combined score on the top line of the chart on page 28.
5. Locate the number that corresponds to your score for Questionnaire #1 on the far left vertical column of the graph.
6. Draw a horizontal line across the page from the Questionnaire #1 score; then draw a vertical line down from the combined score.
7. The number in the box where the two lines intersect is the adjusted percentile score for Questionnaire #1. It indicates your percentage of physical sexuality.
8. Subtract that score from one hundred to determine your percentage of emotional sexuality.

Note: Once you have scored your Sexuality Questionnaires, look ahead to your scores for the Suggestibility Questionnaires at the end of this chapter. If you are physically sexual with more than forty percent physical suggestibility, add ten percent to your degree of emotional sexuality. The rationale behind this is that emotional suggestibility has a tendency to suppress some areas of physical sexuality, causing a person to appear less physically sexual than he or she really is. Likewise, physical suggestibility decreases the manifestations of emotional sexuality, causing a person to appear less emotionally sexual than he or she actually is.

Suggestibility

Earlier we discussed the fact that our sexuality is determined by our secondary caretaker, usually the father. Suggestibility, which reflects the way we learn and also is a factor in how we will utilize self-hypnosis, is also part of our childhood conditioning. However, suggestibility comes from the primary caretaker, usually our mothers.

Suggestibility is actually a defense mechanism to protect us from the pain of rejection when we are small. It comes from the learned ability to interpret the real messages our mothers are giving us as we develop and grow. Only through understanding what our mothers, or

SCORE #1	200	195	190	185	180	175	170	165	160	155	150	145	140	135	130	125	120	115	110	105	100	95	90	85	80	75	70	65	60	55	50
100	50	51	53	54	56	57	59	61	63	64	67	69	71	74	77	80	83	87	91	95	100										
95	48	49	50	51	53	54	56	58	59	61	63	66	68	70	73	76	79	83	86	90	95	100									
90	45	46	47	49	50	51	53	55	56	58	60	62	64	67	69	72	75	78	82	86	90	95	100								
85	43	44	45	46	47	49	50	51	53	55	57	59	61	63	65	70	71	74	77	81	85	89	94	100							
80	40	41	42	43	44	46	47	48	50	52	53	55	57	59	61	64	67	70	73	76	80	84	89	94	100						
75	37	38	39	40	42	43	44	45	47	48	50	52	54	56	58	62	63	65	68	71	75	79	83	88	94	100					
70	35	36	37	38	39	40	41	42	44	45	47	48	50	52	54	56	58	61	64	67	70	74	78	82	88	93	100				
65	33	33	34	35	36	37	38	39	41	42	43	45	46	48	50	52	54	56	59	62	65	68	72	76	81	87	93	100			
60	30	31	32	33	33	34	35	36	38	39	40	41	43	44	46	48	50	52	54	57	60	63	67	71	75	80	86	92	100		
55	28	28	29	30	31	31	32	33	34	35	37	38	39	41	42	44	46	48	50	52	55	58	61	65	69	73	79	85	91	100	
50	25	26	26	27	28	29	29	30	31	32	33	34	36	37	38	40	42	45	45	48	50	53	56	59	63	67	71	77	83	91	100
45	23	23	24	24	25	26	26	27	28	29	30	31	32	33	35	36	38	39	41	43	45	47	50	53	56	60	65	69	75	82	90
40	20	20	22	22	22	23	23	24	25	26	27	28	28	30	31	32	33	35	36	38	40	42	44	47	50	53	57	61	67	73	80
35	18	18	19	19	19	20	21	21	22	23	23	24	25	26	27	28	29	30	32	33	35	37	39	41	44	47	50	54	58	64	70
30	15	15	16	16	17	17	18	18	19	19	20	21	21	22	23	24	25	26	27	29	30	32	33	35	38	40	43	46	50	54	60
25	13	13	13	13	14	14	15	15	16	16	17	17	18	18	19	20	21	22	23	24	25	26	28	29	31	33	36	38	42	45	50
20	10	10	11	11	11	11	12	12	13	13	13	15	15	16	16	16	17	17	18	19	20	21	22	23	25	27	29	31	33	36	40
15	8	8	8	8	8	9	9	9	9	10	10	10	11	11	11	12	13	13	14	14	15	16	17	18	19	20	21	23	25	27	30
10	5	5	5	5	6	6	6	6	6	6	7	7	7	7	8	8	8	9	9	9	10	10	11	12	13	13	14	15	17	18	20
5	3	3	3	3	3	3	3	3	3	3	3	3	4	4	4	4	4	4	5	5	5	5	6	6	6	7	7	8	8	9	10
0	0	0	0	0	0	0	0	0	0	0	0	0	0	0	0	0	0	0	0	0	0	0	0	0	0	0	0	0	0	0	0

SCORE #1

other primary caretakers, truly want from us can we feel comfortable in the relationship we so badly need as children.

For example, suppose you are passing by a playground on a rainy afternoon. There are a few small children and their mothers in the playground, trying to adjust to the intermittent showers.

One mother is wearing old clothes, sitting on the grass with her young child, playing with a small puddle of water. She is taking leaves and twigs, showing her small child how to make tiny boats in the water. When the rain comes, they pretend that the drops striking the water are giant waves. The leaves become ocean liners, tossed by the water, trying to make a safe return to shore. "Isn't this a lovely day?" she says, her child giggling delightedly. "I'm so glad we decided to come here. We'll have to get dry so we don't catch cold when we go home, but isn't this fun?"

A second mother is extremely harried. Her child has been cooped up inside the house much too long and she felt the need to take him to the park. But now it's raining. Her clothing is too nice for such weather and her new hairdo is being damaged. Her child wants to play in the mud but she keeps grabbing his arm and dragging him along. "Isn't this a lovely day?" she says angrily. "I'm so glad we decided to come here." Her voice is dripping with sarcasm and she is determined to get into shelter as soon as possible, even if it means half ripping her son's arm from the socket in an effort to hurry along. "Isn't this fun?"

The words used by both mothers are almost identical, though it is obvious that their meanings are quite different. The one child is learning that his mother means exactly what she says. The mother thinks that it is a fine day because she and her child are having fun in the park. They are sharing an experience which requires the rain to be enjoyed. It is wet, perhaps a little cold, but they are dressed for it and she will make certain that neither stays wet long enough to become ill. The child has learned that his mother means exactly what she says. He also has learned that when he wants to communicate with her, he should do it literally. He will become an adult who says what he means.

The second child is learning that his mother does not say what she means. That mother is also describing a "fine day," but what she really means is that the day is awful. She is miserable, determined to get out of there, and extremely sarcastic. This child has learned that his mother infers messages. She does not say what she means all the time. She often is saying quite the opposite and it is necessary to search for other signals—her tone of voice, the tension of her body, the way she moves—to understand the message. He knows that when talking with her, he may need to hint at his feelings rather than saying exactly what he means.

The way in which a child is disciplined will also affect suggestibility. For example, again we have two children and two mothers. This time the child gets a large ball for a present and is warned not to play with it in the house. Both children disobey, but the mothers act quite differently upon hearing the crash of a favorite lamp knocked from a table by the bouncing ball.

The first mother rushes in, scolds the child, and takes away the ball. She may say something such as: "You disobeyed me. Obviously you are not yet ready to have a toy like this because you choose to play with it inside. I'm going to put this ball away and not give it back to you until I think you are old enough to play with it properly." The child begins crying, upset over the scolding and the loss of a new toy, yet the mother ignores her. She puts the ball on the top shelf of a closet and returns to her chores. The child is left to pout, think about what happened, and then go back to playing. There is no reward for doing wrong and no pleasure from the punishment.

The second mother, experiencing the same situation, rushes in and scolds the child, perhaps giving the child a spanking. This time the child cries and the mother feels either a little guilty or takes the attitude that since the child is crying, she is repentant and forgiveness is essential. The mother returns to the child, taking her in her arms, and comforting her. Perhaps she will rock the child, sing, or gently stroke her forehead. There is great pleasure in this interaction despite the physical discomfort that preceded it.

The first child learns that when you do something wrong, you are punished. There is a direct cause and effect relationship, with no pleasure coming from the pain. The second child learns that when you do something wrong, a pleasurable experience can follow the punishment. This child may find that the most loving attention in his or her life comes from the reward following the pain. It is quite possible that the child will develop the habit of doing something naughty when attention is desired. Then the child will learn to either minimize the discomfort of the punishment or accept it, always in anticipation of the reward.

This second child learns that physical touch is extremely pleasurable. The body can be used for great comfort, and physical touch is a reward. This child will crave the physical touch while the first child sees physical contact as less than pleasurable. Each is naturally responding to the signals provided during childhood, again, usually by the primary caretaker, the mother.

The child also learns to crave physical touching (physical suggestibility) when a mother shows great physical affection and then denies it. For example, suppose a mother has always wanted a child. When she gives birth, she can't seem to get her fill of the new baby. She touches and caresses the infant, strokes the body, and generally expresses love through direct contact.

A year or two passes, during which the family finances begin to change. The father is not making as much money as the family needs and the mother decides to she must go to work. Suddenly, there isn't the time available for the close attention she had been giving her child. There is no longer the intense physical contact to which the child had become accustomed. As a result, the child, and later the adult, will always seek the physical sensations.

An overly protective mother can reinforce this physical suggestibility as well. For example, a mother may constantly call attention to the needs of the body: "Wear your raincoat. If your body gets wet, you'll get a chill." "Better put on your gloves. Your hands will freeze with all that snow." "Are you sure that jacket will be warm enough? You don't want your body to get cold." Each statement makes the child think about his or her body. The demands come so frequently that the child is constantly reminded of the potential problems and is ever alert to physical feelings.

The emotional suggestibility comes from the mother who gives mixed messages. Her statements fail to match what the child perceives to be her real meaning. For example, the woman in the park who was so anxious to flee the rain was making a statement which was quite different from her true feelings. As a result, the child becomes confused and is unable to trust just the verbal messages. He or she must learn to be less influenced by what is said than the potential hidden meanings behind the words.

A slightly different cause of emotional suggestibility comes from the woman who smothers her child with physical attention. She is constantly grabbing and hugging the child when the child is not seeking attention. The child may be playing quietly with some toys, carrying on a game which he or she finds totally absorbing. Suddenly the mother rushes over and says, "You look so adorable when you're playing. I could just love you to pieces." Then she hugs and kisses the child, interrupting the game and thoroughly disgusting the child who simply wants to be left alone at that moment.

Over time, that smothering with attention makes the child withdraw from the physical contact. He or she learns to ignore the parent's touch most of the time. The child learns to develop strong emotions, such as anger, when there is a chance of physical touching.

The same is true for a child who is spanked without an immediate reward. Touching means pain and the angry parent is one who generates fear. The child tenses, not wanting to be touched. Again, this strengthens the emotional suggestibility of the child.

The mother of an emotional suggestible has spoken literally but inferred a different message, which the child is trying to understand. This usually occurs during the years from two to five when a child is becoming aware of others, both adults and children. His or her ability to communicate changes because children and adults outside the immediate family make little or no effort to understand the child. The child is instead expected to adapt to others. Again, this requires an ability to read inferences in others to some degree.

The child will also learn to adapt to the father in ways that may be different from his mother. For example, when a father is an emotional sexual and the mother is a physical sexual, the child must learn to communicate inferentially to the father. Otherwise there can be a problem. The father might say, "Will you tell me your name?" If this is said to a literal child, he or she will say, "Yes." If this is said to an inferred child, the child will say, "My name is Johnny." Yet saying "Yes" to the father, although an exact response to the question, could result in the father's becoming angry. The child thus learns to respond inferentially, giving his or her name, when the more natural (for that child) literal response seemed, at first, to be appropriate.

Another situation is when a parent enters a room in which there are toys scattered all over the floor. The parent may say, "This floor is a mess. The toys should be picked up." The literal child's response will be, "Yes, they should be picked up." The inferred child will understand the implications of the statement and begin picking up the toys.

Suggestibility, unlike sexuality, may readily be balanced for a child. For example, a mother may provide moderate discipline without a rewarding hug to stop the tears (emotional suggestible) but also provide enough touching and physical reassurance at other times to create comfort with touch (physical suggestible). This balance leads to an adult who is comfortable with both forms of suggestibility, even though the sexuality may remain strongly emotional or physical because of the relationship with the father.

Suggestibility may also be created by parents who are inconsistent in their behavior patterns. A child who is punished and ignored for causing a problem one day, then punished and rewarded with touching the next time he or she acts in the same manner, will develop an ambiguity. The child will come to respond with an even suggestibility just because of the confusion generated.

The suggestibility is strengthened when a child goes to school or day care for the first time. Young children have no sense of others. They are extremely self-centered and only understand their own feelings. They do not worry about what another child is thinking. Thus, when they have experiences, they tend to react in whatever way is most comfortable for them. This may mean constant physical confrontations with peers and teachers or it may mean a quiet withdrawal, feeling emotions and avoiding the touch. They avoid anything which might call attention to their physical bodies and use their emotional responses to cope.

Adults do not follow the same rigidity as children. Their greater understanding of others and ability to change results in a constant state of fluctuation. Rarely will they alter their created sexuality, such as going from emotional to physical, but the degree of emotional or physical suggestibility will change.

The following test will help you determine your suggestibility. Again, remember that there is no right or wrong no matter how you score. By knowing your suggestibility, you will be able to use the information to help yourself change your sex life for the better. This knowledge will be especially helpful with self-hypnosis since the way you think about yourself and others must be understood in order for you to grow in your relationships. It is the combination of physical and emotional suggestibility that makes you what you are and determines the course of your sex life.

Answer all questions of both questionnaires before scoring.

SUGGESTIBILITY QUESTIONNAIRE #1

1. Have you ever walked in your sleep during your adult life?
2. As a teenager, did you feel comfortable expressing your feelings to one or both of your parents?
3. Do you have a tendency to look directly into people's eyes and/or move closely to them when discussing an interesting subject?
4. Do you feel that most people you meet for the first time are uncritical of your appearance?
5. In a group situation with people you have just met, would you feel comfortable drawing attention to yourself by initiating a conversation?
6. Do you feel comfortable holding hands or hugging someone you are in a relationship with while other people are present?
7. When someone talks about feeling warm physically, do you begin to feel warm also?
8. Do you occasionally have a tendency to tune out when someone is talking to you, and at times not even hear what the other person is saying, because you are anxious to come up with your side of it?
9. Do you feel that you learn and comprehend better by seeing and/or reading than by hearing?
10. In a new class or lecture situation, do you usually feel comfortable asking questions in front of the group?
11. When expressing your ideas, do you find it important to relate all the details leading up to the subject so the other person can understand it completely?
12. Do you enjoy relating to children?
13. Do you find it easy to be at ease and comfortable with your body movements, even when faced with unfamiliar people and circumstances?
14. Do you prefer reading fiction rather than nonfiction?
15. If you were to imagine sucking a sour, bitter, juicy, yellow lemon, would your mouth water?
16. If you feel that you deserve to be complimented for something well done, do you feel comfortable if the compliment is given to you in front of other people?
17. Do you feel that you are a good conversationalist?
18. Do you feel comfortable when complimentary attention is drawn to your physical body or appearance?

SUGGESTIBILITY QUESTIONNAIRE #2

1. Have you ever awakened in the middle of the night and felt that you could not move your body and/or could not talk?

2. As a child, did you feel that you were more affected by the tone of voice of your parents than by what they actually said?

3. If someone you are associated with talks about a fear that you too have experienced, do you have a tendency to have an apprehensive or fearful feeling also?

4. After an argument is over, do you have a tendency to dwell on what you could or should have said?

5. Do you have a tendency to tune out occasionally when someone is talking to you—perhaps not even hear what was said—because your mind has drifted to something totally unrelated?

6. Do you sometimes desire to be complimented for a job well done, but feel embarrassed or uncomfortable when complimented?

7. Do you often have a fear or dread of not being able to carry on a conversation with someone you have just met?

8. Do you feel self-conscious when attention is drawn to your physical body or appearance?

9. If you have your choice, would you rather avoid being around children most of the time?

10. Do you feel that you are not relaxed or loose in body movements, especially when faced with unfamiliar people or circumstances?

11. Do you prefer reading nonfiction rather than fiction?

12. If someone describes a very bitter taste, do you have difficulty experiencing the physical feeling of it?

13. Do you generally feel that you see yourself less favorably than others see you?

14. Do you tend to feel awkward or self-conscious initiating touch (holding hands, kissing, and the like) with someone you are in a relationship with while other people are present?

15. In a new class or lecture situation, do you usually feel uncomfortable asking questions in front of the group even though you may desire further explanation?

16. Do you feel uneasy if someone you have just met looks you directly in the eyes when talking to you, especially if the conversation is about you?

17. In a group situation with people you have just met, would you feel uncomfortable drawing attention to yourself by initiating a conversation?

18. If you are in a relationship or are very close to someone, do you find it difficult or embarrassing to verbalize your love for him or her?

SCORING INSTRUCTIONS
FOR SUGGESTIBILITY QUESTIONNAIRES

1. Count the number of *yes* answers on Questionnaire #1. Give yourself five points for each *yes* answer to questions 3 through 18 and ten points for each *yes* answer to questions 1 and 2.
2. Do the same for Questionnaire #2.
3. Add the two scores together to obtain the combined score.
4. Locate your combined score number on the top horizontal line of the graph.
5. Locate the number that corresponds to your score for Questionnaire #1 on the far left vertical column of the graph.
6. Draw a horizontal line across the page from the Questionnaire #1 score; then draw a vertical line down from the combined score.
7. The number in the box where the two lines intersect is the adjusted percentile score for Questionnaire #1. It indicates your percentage of physical suggestibility. It indicates your percentage of physical suggestibility.
8. Subtract that score from one hundred to determine your percentage of emotional suggestibility.

SCORE #1	200	195	190	185	180	175	170	165	160	155	150	145	140	135	130	125	120	115	110	105	100	95	90	85	80	75	70	65	60	55	50
100	50	51	53	54	56	57	59	61	63	64	67	69	71	74	77	80	83	87	91	95	100										
95	48	49	50	51	53	54	56	58	59	61	63	66	68	70	73	76	79	83	86	90	95	100									
90	45	46	47	49	50	51	53	55	56	58	60	62	64	67	69	72	75	78	82	86	90	95	100								
85	43	44	45	46	47	49	50	51	53	55	57	59	61	63	65	70	71	74	77	81	85	89	94	100							
80	40	41	42	43	44	46	47	48	50	52	53	55	57	59	61	64	67	70	73	76	80	84	89	94	100						
75	37	38	39	40	42	43	44	45	47	48	50	52	54	56	58	62	63	65	68	71	75	79	83	88	94	100					
70	35	36	37	38	39	40	41	42	44	45	47	48	50	52	54	56	58	61	64	67	70	74	78	82	88	93	100				
65	33	33	34	35	36	37	38	39	41	42	43	45	46	48	50	52	54	56	59	62	65	68	72	76	81	87	93	100			
60	30	31	32	33	33	34	35	36	38	39	40	41	43	44	46	48	50	52	54	57	60	63	67	71	75	80	86	92	100		
55	28	28	29	30	31	31	32	33	34	35	37	38	39	41	42	44	46	48	50	52	55	58	61	65	69	73	79	85	91	100	
50	25	26	26	27	28	29	29	30	31	32	33	34	36	37	38	40	42	45	45	48	50	53	56	59	63	67	71	77	83	91	100
45	23	23	24	24	25	26	26	27	28	29	30	31	32	33	35	36	38	39	41	43	45	47	50	53	56	60	65	69	75	82	90
40	20	20	22	22	22	23	23	24	25	26	27	28	28	30	31	32	33	35	36	38	40	42	44	47	50	53	57	61	67	73	80
35	18	18	19	19	19	20	21	21	22	23	23	24	25	26	27	28	29	30	32	33	35	37	39	41	44	47	50	54	58	64	70
30	15	15	16	16	17	17	18	18	19	19	20	21	21	22	23	24	25	26	27	29	30	32	33	35	38	40	43	46	50	54	60
25	13	13	13	13	14	14	15	15	16	16	17	17	18	18	19	20	21	22	23	24	25	26	28	21	31	33	36	38	42	45	50
20	10	10	11	11	11	11	12	12	13	13	13	15	15	16	16	16	17	17	18	19	20	21	22	23	25	27	29	31	33	36	40
15	8	8	8	8	8	9	9	9	9	10	10	10	11	11	11	12	13	13	14	14	15	16	17	18	19	20	21	23	25	27	30
10	5	5	5	5	6	6	6	6	6	6	7	7	7	7	8	8	8	9	9	9	10	10	11	12	13	13	14	15	17	18	20
5	3	3	3	3	3	3	3	3	3	3	3	3	4	4	4	4	4	4	5	5	5	5	6	6	6	7	7	8	8	9	10
0	0	0	0	0	0	0	0	0	0	0	0	0	0	0	0	0	0	0	0	0	0	0	0	0	0	0	0	0	0	0	0

Sex and self-hypnosis

3

What can I say? I like women. I work as the sales manager of the appliance department and I try to dress in a way that catches the eye. Appearance is important, you know, and if the women don't think I'm a sharp dresser, they're going to be a little turned off when I approach them about buying a stereo or refrigerator or whatever.

Besides, they turn me on. Do you know what it's like to smell their perfume, to brush against them when I'm going over the warranty and the contracts? I think half of my day is spent fantasizing about taking them over to the furniture department and doing it right there on one of the beds. My girl friends are always satisfied because I can go again and again. I mean, wouldn't you with all that stimulation all day?

Craig, a highly successful salesman,
discussing how he thinks about sex.

I've got to get in the mood. I'm an executive secretary for the head of a manufacturing plant and there are endless details I have to handle for my boss each day. I'm forever arranging conferences, planning flight schedules, going over the records, and handling all the other tasks which seem to be never-ending in this type of job.

When I go home, sex is the last thing on my mind. I want to relax, maybe take a hot bath and just soak my body. Then it's kind of nice to have my back rubbed, to feel my neck being stroked, perhaps to sit and listen to music while leaning against my boy friend's shoulder. I know he's probably ready to go at it, but I don't always want that. Sometimes I just want the feeling of closeness. Eventually we usually end up in bed together, but it's not my top priority. If he tries to rush things, I just can't seem to get very excited. It's just nice to ease into it the way most people do. Don't you think so?

Anna, discussing how
she approaches a sexual relationship.

Two different people; two different sexual needs. Each thinks the feelings experienced in preparation for the sex act are typical of everyone else, yet each is quite different. What they do share is the use of a form of self-hypnotic suggestion to prepare themselves for the sex act.

Self-hypnosis is actually a mental process involving the focusing of your attention on a particular subject. For example, remember when you were in school, studying for a test and scared that you would have problems? You forced yourself to concentrate, determined to learn the material. You knew that if you applied your thinking, you would be fine, so you focused on the subject, excluding all else.

Then came the day of the exam. Again you were frightened, this time concerned that you would not remember what you had tried so hard to learn. As you walked into class, you attempted a mental review, then panicked because nothing would come back.

Finally, almost certain you were going to fail, you nervously sat down. The moment you looked at the test, all the material you thought you had forgotten suddenly returned to mind. You were able to focus upon the questions and answer them effectively.

The sex act is a natural self-hypnotic process which begins with the fantasy stage and continues with a narrowing of focus until orgasm or climax. Whenever we break this narrowing of focus, such as through fear, guilt, anger, or a partner acting in a manner which does not satisfy our needs, then we have difficulty with sex. Once we understand how to more effectively use this natural process, often instituting it before the sex act to more easily become aroused, then there is little or no difficulty encountered.

The Suggestibility Factor

As you learned in Chapter 2, the desire for sex will vary with the individual. Physical sexuals have a greater desire for sex than their emotional counterparts. Many physical sexuals want sex the moment they awaken in the morning and before they go to sleep at night. They will also enjoy time in bed at any hour in between when the circumstances are right.

An emotional sexual, on the other hand, may have the strongest desire for sex on a cyclical basis. Thus the individual may go from twenty-four to seventy-two hours without an intense sex drive. This does not mean that he or she is undersexed; many emotional sexuals can enjoy sex almost as much as their particular physical sexual partner. They have to be brought to the desire more slowly when the sex act is enjoyed other than during their most intense periods of sexual drive. Without patient encouragement, the emotional sexual will routinely seek sex no more than two to three times a week. A physical sexual partner who understands the emotional sexual needs can help the emotional sexual increase the frequency of sexual activity. Yet even with this assistance, an emotional sexual will never have the desire for sex that is found with the physical sexual.

Yet even within these variances, the suggestibility factor of the individual plays the greatest role in the sex drive. The higher your physical suggestibility score, the more you are going to desire sex. Thus a physical sexual with a low physical suggestibility score is going to want sex with much less frequency than an emotional sexual with a very high physical suggestibility score.

Len is typical of the extreme physical sexual with a strong physical suggestibility. When he took the tests in the previous chapter, he scored eighty percent on each. He came to see me because he felt he was oversexed, a fact which had cost him two wives, several girl friends, and the wrath of co-workers whom he regularly tried to seduce.

Len was constantly aware of his bodily sensations. He was a track and field star in high school, eventually becoming quite successful in college competition in the United States. Even in his early thirties, he continued long-distance running, weekly basketball games, and other physical activities. He was constantly watching his weight and his health, aware of every physical sensation as he attempted to keep himself in top condition.

Len also worked extensively on the job. He was a contractor with a successful company, but he most enjoyed getting out on the job and working with the men and women on the job site. He told me that just watching some of the women he employed would get him excited.

> I never thought a man could go too far with sex, but I think something's wrong. I've had sex with my wife in the morning, taken one of the girls at the office for a quickie over lunch time, and then, while paying for whatever food we grab on the way back to the office, try to pick up the waitress for when she gets off duty. I'm always on the prowl and somehow that doesn't seem as much fun as it once did.

The reality for Len was that he was in a constant state of self-hypnosis related to sex. He was extremely suggestible and let all manner of signals get him aroused. A woman's body, a friendly female smile, or almost anything else would immediately remind him of sex. Since he was also a physical suggestible, his immediate reaction was to want to go to bed with her right then. Thus he combined a strong physical sexuality with what amounts to a perpetual state of self-hypnosis in which he focused only on sex. It was no wonder he felt that he was behaving in the extreme.

There are many men and women like Len, and they are quite easy to help. Since they already are experiencing high suggestibility, they are perpetually in the fantasy stage of the sex act, as described in Chapter 2. All they have to do is learn to rechannel their thought process to nonsexual stimulation whenever such sexual desires are inappropriate. They are using the self-hypnosis they already are experiencing with their high physical suggestibility and desensitizing the sex drive when it is not appropriate. Thus they lose such intensity and are able to maintain more stable relationships with their spouses or lovers.

An emotional sexual can also be a high physical suggestible. Karen was such an individual and her problem was what some people call nymphomania. She worked as a bookkeeper for a department store and came to see me because she felt herself unable to have a satisfactory relationship.

> I guess I'm a romantic. I like to read novels in which the heroine is carried off on a pirate ship or to some mysterious castle. I like to fantasize that I'm being taken away for a sexual rendezvous with a stranger I'll grow to love. It's rape but it's something I want.
>
> When I'm at work, it seems as though everything reminds me of sex. I'll smell a man's cologne and imagine what that would be like with him in bed. Or one of the men will walk around with his tie loose and his shirt slightly unbuttoned so I can see his chest, and I'll imagine what he's like naked.
>
> If I go on a date to a restaurant, I'll fantasize that whatever we're talking about is actually his way of seducing me. I've even done this during business lunches when I know better, yet by the time we're done eating, I've lubricated and am ready to jump into bed with the first person who offers.
>
> Yet when I do go to bed with a man, and I'm quite experienced, it's never very satisfactory. Maybe he's too fast or too clumsy or, I don't know what. He just doesn't match up to my expectations and I'm always left feeling a little disappointed. It's like I'm determined to try again as soon as possible because I know that the next man is going to measure up to my hopes. But they never do. They never seem to be as good as I expect.

Karen was typical of the person whose sexuality is emotional but who has a high physical suggestibility rating. Again, she is in the fantasy stage of sex, her mind focusing on those ideas which she finds erotically stimulating. She is also keeping herself in self-hypnosis, maintaining an ongoing sex drive.

The problem Karen faces, along with all the other men and women who are like her, is the fact that the emotional sexual needs slower physical stimulation. The fact that she is highly excited from the fantasy stage does not mean that her body has warmed for the act or that she is ready for immediate intercourse. She still requires the slower touching process, usually with the early stimulation well away from the genitals, in order to be truly ready for orgasm. Yet because of the high fantasy excitation, she has a tendency to go to bed immediately, having intercourse which is not satisfactory for her. She is frustrated, then becomes aroused through the fantasy stage, and wants to try again.

This type of woman is often called a nymphomaniac, though men can experience this same problem. Again, the solution will involve an awareness of the self-hypnotic state, in part to reduce the constant fantasizing and in part to learn how to prolong the touching necessary for an emotional sexual to have a satisfactory sex act.

Remember that the physical sexual is highly receptive to touch while the emotional sexual is not very receptive to touch. This does not change just because there is a high physical suggestibility present. Yet the emotional sexual with a high physical suggestibility will often move too fast for a satisfactory relationship. The physical sexual who is also physically suggestible will not have this problem. The suggestibility simply enhances the desire for action.

Note: The amount of sex in which a man or woman engages, both through masturbation and with a sex partner, is determined by suggestibility. The quality of that sex is determined by the way in which the needs of his or her sexuality are met during the sex act. A physical sexual who has an extreme emotional suggestibility has at least one third the desire for sex as the physical sexual who is also a physical suggestible. Yet both may enjoy the actual sex act equally.

Suggestibility is how we learn. Sexuality is how we practice what we learn.

It is fairly easy to spot the types of individuals who fall into these categories because all of us tend to engage in activities which relate to our sexuality. For example, the male physical sexual is concerned about his appearance. He may enjoy body building, seek clothing which enhances his appearance, and act in a way which he feels is manly.

The physical sexual is usually quite outgoing and does well in jobs such as sales. He is often aggressive and comfortable directing people. However, he is generally poor with details and tends to be disorganized when it comes to paperwork. Such an individual usually requires an assistant to handle all the details of whatever he is doing.

The physical sexual female is equally concerned with her body and appearance. She, like the physical sexual male, prefers sports cars which enhance her appearance. She is also the type to move up in an organization, becoming a top executive. She will be dynamic, excellent in sales, and also rather disorganized.

Makeup, perfume, and hair styles will be carefully planned by the physical sexual female. She is likely to be highly successful in upper management where others can handle the detail work.

Both the physical sexual male and female, when high physical suggestible, are easily turned on by looks. They seek the subtle eye play that can hint of sexual desire or just approval of the way they look when attending social gatherings. Both will tend to look at crotches, seeing the opposite sex below the waist before noticing the rest of the body.

This type of man and woman will relate sex and love. They are not the types for casual affairs, falling in love with each bedmate who arouses them. They may engage in one night stands, but they are uncomfortable the next day. If they enjoyed the time in bed, they want to go back to that partner again and again. To them, an enjoyable sex act means that they are in love. The fact that the relationship may not have advanced anywhere close to the degree where the emotional sexual partner is ready to consider any form of commitment is not comprehensible to them. They fall in love and are easily hurt by any hint of rejection even when the relationship was meant to be a casual experience. They want to keep calling the other person and are deeply hurt if the other person does not contact them should such a contact have been expected.

These individuals also enjoy verbal voyeurism. A direct sexual overture in an appropriate situation will excite them. However, when these overtures vary from conservative approaches, they may not be comfortable. For example, a suggestion for any type of variation, such as oral intercourse, will be a turn-off. They are rather conservative and prefer straight intercourse, usually with the missionary position.

The complete opposites are the emotional sexuals who are also emotional suggestible. These are individuals who are not particularly interested in sex. They require subtle seduction to slowly work themselves into sex. In fact, the physical partner may have to take control of the relationship, gradually working the partner into the mood through indirect suggestion and subtle cues, such as the touch of a hand while at dinner. However, once the fantasy of sex has been adequately stimulated, they will be as aroused as the physical partner.

The emotionals often explain that they lack a strong interest in sex. It is not a high priority. They are comfortable involving themselves with work and family activities which have nothing to do with sex. It is not that they are frigid; it is just that they are not obtaining sexual clues from their surroundings as the physical sexual, physical suggestible will do. In that same business conference where the physical suggestible female is letting the sights, smells, and sounds all help her focus on sex, the emotional suggestible is paying attention to the business. The emotional sexual may also be using self-hypnosis to focus attention, but the focus is on the work at hand, not the sexual clues coming from the interaction of the men and women present.

The emotional sexual female is often the type who seeks jobs that place her as the power behind the throne. Instead of being outgoing and trying to lead an organization, she will be the executive secretary or the administrative assistant. Her pleasure and skill will come from attention to details. She will enjoy turning ideas into practice. She may be extremely well-paid and quite literally run a company that is headed by a physical sexual, physical suggestible, but all the manipulation will be behind the scenes.

The emotional sexual male or female may also take jobs that require great attention to detail, such as accounting and legal research. When they enter an elite field, such as politics, they eventually work into power behind the scenes. These are the individuals you seldom hear about, the power brokers who have subtle pressure but are not in the newspapers all the time. The Speaker of the House may be someone who is an emotional suggestible, working behind the scenes to consolidate power, letting others stay in the spotlight of the media.

Emotional sexuals who are emotional suggestible will make poor sales personnel and tend to dress extremely conservatively. They do not want to call attention to their bodies and, in an ongoing relationship, having sex once or twice a week fits their normal desires. Naturally, with an understanding partner, they can be mentally stimulated more frequently, encouraging the fantasy stage so their desire is greater. However, the partner does have to initiate this change.

Again, all of these individuals are using self-hypnosis, either as a turn-on or a turn-off. The problem is that it is not channeled according to the needs of their relationship. They are unaware of their potential control and the ways in which they can improve their enjoyment of the sex act. It is self-hypnosis without direction.

How Self-Hypnosis Becomes Destructive

Unless you understand that all of us use self-hypnosis in our relationships, there is a point where a couple begins to use it the wrong way without realizing they are doing so. For example, there is the case of

Mark and Brenda, a couple in their late twenties who had been married
for three years. Mark was a tax lawyer with a large corporation. He was
one of several such individuals on the staff and worked a traditional
nine-to-five day. Brenda was a manufacturer's representative who
frequently traveled to conventions and client stores in order to sell the
company's products. She explained:

> I don't know what's wrong. When we were first married, we used to have
> sex every day. I traveled a lot, but every night I'd call Mark and tell him all
> the things I was looking forward to doing with him when I returned. The
> moment I got back, he'd pick me up at the airport and we'd neck like
> teenagers all the way to our apartment. Then I'd sit on his lap, kissing him
> and telling him about my week, and then we'd tumble into bed.
>
> I had to stop all the telephone calls after a while because the expense
> was just too great. They weren't covered by my employer and we couldn't
> handle the cost. I'd still be met at the airport and Mark would still take me
> to bed when we got finished saying our hellos, but often that would be it.
> We might have sex the next day and we might not. It was as though
> Mark's desires were satisfied with that one time, and I wanted to go to bed
> with him again and again until I had to fly off again.
>
> For a while I worried that he had a mistress. I suspected some of the
> women who worked in the legal division of his company. If we went to a
> party with them, I'd be watching for any signs of a relationship. But I
> never did see any proof that that was going on. Yet Mark just didn't make
> sense to me. It was as though he was falling out of love with me.

Mark did not see life quite the way Brenda did.

> I don't know why she's so upset, Dr. Kappas. I adore my wife and I'm
> delighted with her success. I would never cheat on her because I know
> that I could never find someone I could love as much.
>
> I guess Brenda just doesn't understand that you can't keep on the
> honeymoon forever. She has her life flying around the country and I've
> tried to develop interests to keep me occupied when she's gone. I started
> collecting stamps and really enjoy doing research and attending the
> stamp shows. I've tried to get involved in an occasional community
> activity as well, figuring that we could go to the meetings together when
> Brenda's home. I've been trying to build a normal life and that means I'm
> just not thinking about sex all the time. I enjoy my sex life with her. I don't
> understand what the problem is.

There were several factors at work in this situation. First, there was the natural attraction of opposites, though this was not a serious problem. Certainly their drives and needs were different, but both Mark and Brenda were anxious to make their marriage work. They were willing to compromise in any way necessary to stay together.

The second factor was the way in which they began using the natural self-hypnosis of the human mind. Brenda enjoyed staying in a high excitation fantasy stage concerning Mark when she traveled. If she walked by a department store displaying clothing, she thought how sexy Mark would look in it. When she went to bed in a hotel room, she thought of the things she and Mark could be doing if he was there. If she dozed on the plane, she would use those moments before going to sleep to think about the welcome she would receive and what it would be like to touch Mark's naked body once again.

Mark, on the other hand, did not want to be constantly aroused. He knew he couldn't act out sexual fantasy, so he saw no point in mentally arousing himself. Instead, he busied himself with his hobbies and his work. He began concentrating on shows he would attend, usually with Brenda on his arm but in a nonsexual context. He deliberately avoided the fantasy stage of sex, letting himself begin to be aroused only when she was back and taking the initiative.

After the first day, Brenda remained in high sexual excitation because she was constantly keeping herself suggestible to sex. Mark, on the other hand, had redirected his suggestibility so that he was constantly thinking about everything else. What had been a mechanism to fight loneliness was now an automatic withdrawal. Brenda expected him to make the first moves after she had been so aggressive each time she returned, but he was no longer in the same frame of mind. He needed her encouragement to start his fantasy stage of sex and she could not understand this. Each thought the other must be identical in the way they thought. Thus Brenda felt that Mark must be fantasizing about another woman and Mark assumed that Brenda was concentrating on nonsexual areas after she returned. Each waited for the other to make the first move and the result was constant friction.

By understanding your suggestibility, you can take control of your relationship in order to improve your sex life. You will be able to use self-hypnosis to control both your arousal and your orgasm. You will also be able to adjust your sex life so that it is mutual in terms of desire, frequency, and quality.

The Two Types of Sexual Release

The term *orgasm* in reference to a woman's sexual release is actually an incorrect term. Most women do not have an orgasm, and this is not because of sexual problems. In fact, researchers feel that only thirty percent to forty percent of all women actually achieve the rolling, wave-like sensation that is orgasm.

The reason for this situation is that women frequently achieve climax, not orgasm. Climax is the end of sexual stimulation and excitation. It is a natural way to end the sex act, as natural as the orgasm, and completely rewarding in itself for those women who experience it. The intensity of the climax and the duration of the sensation are much shorter than with orgasm, and this can be a minor disappointment for some women. However, moving from climax to orgasm is extremely easy through the use of self-hypnosis to control the sensation. In fact, a woman who achieves vaginal orgasm can use self-hypnosis to transfer sensations and achieve clitoral orgasm instead.

Some women are unable to achieve either climax or orgasm, a problem caused by subconscious control by past experience. This often relates to past training and feelings of guilt, problems discussed in the next chapter. These are easily overcome with self-hypnosis so that you can enjoy the fullest, most natural expression of sexual fulfillment.

Self-Hypnosis and Your Suggestibility

As you have seen, self-hypnosis is actually an extension of your own suggestibility. It is the mechanism you use to influence your own suggestibility. By entering into a state of self-hypnosis before or during the sex act, you control your thoughts, feelings, and eventual reactions. You are able to eliminate problems and adjust your reactions to your partner so that you have a mutually satisfactory relationship.

Your suggestibility rating is something which is not all-inclusive. If you are eighty percent suggestible according to the test in Chapter 2, this does not mean that you are eighty percent suggestible to everything. When you walk down a busy city street, for example, all manner of stimuli fight for your attention. There are cars moving past, children playing near an alley, business people rushing to and from offices, a policeman directing traffic, neon signs flashing messages, drawings scrawled on walls, and numerous other events. You are aware of everything to one degree or another, of course, but your mind is not focused on it all. You might be paying closest attention to building names and addresses as you look for a specific location. Or you might be noticing members of the opposite sex, thinking about picking someone up for a date, either real or imagined. Or you might be crossing the street against the light, your total attention influenced only by the flow of traffic and the possibility that one of the cars may come too close.

You are naturally using the suggestibility you have when you are engaged in the sex act, yet even then you can be distracted. For example, you might be about to have sex with someone you know casually, even though you were raised to believe that sex was only for marriage and the creation of children. Everything seems right, your mood is romantic, your desire great, yet suddenly you remember all the training from the past. You know in your own mind that you are doing nothing wrong, but that early conditioning causes you to suddenly have problems. This might mean loss of erection or premature ejaculation for a man and failure to lubricate or climax for a woman.

With self-hypnosis, you become suggestible to everything. In this state, you can influence your entire thought process and physical reactions. You can eliminate those subconscious problems and keep yourself suggestible only to the positive aspects of the sex relationship. The self-hypnosis becomes the tool you use to take control of your sex life, making it the most exciting and fulfilling experience possible.

For example, suppose that you are quickly aroused in the fantasy stage of sex. This may occur because you have been thinking about your partner for a prolonged period. It may come from something you have read or seen which put you in the mood. It might have to do with something your partner has said or what your partner is wearing. However it starts, you are now ready to go to the second stage where physical sensation occurs.

One problem that arises for some individuals is that they are very slow to make this transfer from the fantasy stage to the physical stage. This slowness usually goes beyond the typical contrast between the physical and emotional individuals. The transfer takes so long that both partners are frustrated.

The person who has trouble making this transfer can put himself or herself into a state of self-hypnosis during the fantasy stage. Then, he or she mentally creates the physical sensations necessary to enjoy the sex act. With self-hypnosis, there will be a raising of the body temperature, an increased sensitivity to touch in the genital region, perhaps even the earlier lubrication of the female if she has had a problem. You heighten the physical awareness of your body so that you are ready for intercourse at the same time as your partner.

The same situation is used by the woman with sexual problems. Some women have a fear of intercourse coupled with the desire. This usually comes from past training, such as being taught as a young girl that intercourse was dirty, can lead to disease, or is otherwise wrong. Each time such a woman starts to have sex with a man she loves, the subconscious programming forces her to stop. Since this is not a conscious decision, she transfers this fear to a control, causing her to tighten muscles to prevent penetration or keep her from lubricating. This type of woman can use self-hypnosis during the fantasy stage, reminding herself that the sex act is proper, that there is nothing wrong, and gradually decreasing the past influence. At the same time, she is preparing her body with a suggestion that she will lubricate, relax her muscles, and enjoy the penetration. Thus the action which left her a helpless victim, suffering when attempting to have intercourse in the past, is now rechanneled for enjoyment. She uses self-hypnosis to take conscious control of her sexual experience.

Self-hypnosis will enable you to create a positive relationship, no matter what your problem. You will be able to create the condition necessary to change your sex life for the better.

But before we explore the specific ways for you to induce self-hypnosis and the techniques you will use to counter any problems and heighten sexual enjoyment, let us see some of the problems that so many people face. By understanding the typical problems both men and women experience during sex, as well as their causes, it will be easier for you to adapt the self-hypnosis techniques to your specific need.

Common sex problems and their causes

4

There are numerous sexual problems that arise for almost everyone and the results can be heartbreaking. They range from a loss of self-confidence to the break-up of a relationship. This chapter will start with the most frequent problems reported to therapists and continue with some of the lesser understood areas which may be affecting you. Then, in Chapter 5, you will learn the self-hypnosis methods which will enable you to completely overcome your difficulties.

If you are not having problems with your sex life, you will still find that this chapter gives you insight into factors affecting the sex lives of others. Later in this book, there is a chapter discussing ways to improve your sex life, no matter how enjoyable it might already be. That chapter will be of help whether you are young and just learning the full range of sexual expression or elderly and interested in improving sex in your later years.

Both men and women have problems with sex as the result of many factors in their pasts. However, problems are more obvious with the male because it is impossible to fake an erection. The most common difficulty experienced by a male is premature ejaculation. The man reaches orgasm at the moment of penetration, before the woman can be satisfied. George, an independent trucker handling long-distance hauling for a number of companies, explains:

> I don't know what's wrong with me. I have no problem getting it up. If anything, it's just the opposite. I was a football player in high school and had all the girls I wanted. I guess I tried to go through half the girls in my graduating class and had a good share of them actually put out. I've done it in the living rooms with their parents upstairs, in the back of one of those big old Chevies I bought tenth-hand, and even behind the auditorium curtains in school one morning.
>
> But recently I've been serious about just one woman and everything about our relationship is perfect. The trouble is, I come almost the minute I enter her. There isn't time to do anything else, so she never gets satisfied. She says it's okay and I try to manually stimulate her afterwards, but it's not the same. I know she's frustrated and I can see her leaving me soon if I can't learn to hold it longer. Every time I think about going to bed with her and trying to hold my erection longer, I just get turned on more and lose it faster.

George's problem is an extremely common one, though there are several different reasons. In his situation, the difficulty came from both the frequency of early sex and the way in which he had it.

There is nothing romantic about most teenage sexual experiences. Instead of having a strong emotional involvement, the act of desire is confused with love. Boys think that because a girl gets them aroused, they must be in love with her. They do not know that there is a difference between sex and love. Love without sex can be a miserable experience, but sex without love is quite easy to enjoy. The sex act is an enjoyable mental and physical experience which does not require commitment to enjoy. Engaging in sex without deep emotional involvement may be considered taboo by some but that does not change the innate pleasure of the sex act.

Boys like George who have sex frequently, but in circumstances where they fear getting caught, may develop a subconscious attitude that sex must be enjoyed quickly or you will get into trouble. This is then carried over into adult life without the man realizing that fact. The sex act which could have caused him trouble as a teenager is quite different from the circumstances of sex as an adult, though George never made this subconscious transition.

The way in which George learned to have sex was also rather haphazard. Sometimes there was adequate foreplay so that both George and the girls he was dating in high school could achieve release. Other times, it was quite likely that George was the only one satisfied. At that age, there is little awareness of the true needs of a sex partner. It is also unlikely that the girl will talk about being dissatisfied. She would be too young and inexperienced to fully understand the sharing nature of the sex act.

Once George grew older and entered into a more serious, stable relationship, everything changed. He had his own apartment and there was no longer a fear of getting caught. Sex could be savored, the full relationship enjoyed, rather than just an effort to score. Yet subconsciously George was still carrying the fears of adolescence. He had to hurry or get caught. Orgasm became the primary focus of the subconscious mind because there was a chance he would have to stop before release if he did not hurry.

The fact that the reality had changed did not alter this subconscious conditioning. Stopping the premature release was simply a matter of reprogramming the subconscious mind to prolong the enjoyment and insure that he could bring his partner to an effective release.

Extensive masturbation also can lead to premature ejaculation. Typically a boy will fantasize while masturbating. He is thinking about one of the girls in school, someone whose picture he has seen in a magazine, a movie star, or some other female. In his mind, the relationship is a full one, the two of them engaging in whatever foreplay his limited experience allows him to imagine. Finally, he fantasizes penetration at the same time he reaches orgasm. In his mind, both he and the girl are achieving a delightful experience simultaneously.

Eventually the youth reaches a circumstance where he has a serious, ongoing relationship with a real woman. But his subconscious mind is still back in the sexual fantasy stage. He has come to relate penetration with mutual release when, in reality, penetration is the first phase of release for the woman. She must then be stimulated to orgasm by the penis. The woman is not the fantasy of his days of masturbation but he has difficulty keeping from having an orgasm immediately upon penetration.

Both these types of premature ejaculation are quite easily corrected with a similar procedure. This involves the changing of the subconscious mind so that the sex act is more in tune with the reality of mutual needs.

There are other reasons for premature ejaculation by the male, of course. Guilt is often a major problem. A man is raised to feel that sex must only involve procreation, not pleasure. Or the man may have been taught that sex outside of marriage is wrong. Or the man may be involved with the "wrong" woman, someone who does not match the social background, religious background, or some other arbitrary standard he was raised to believe was proper for the woman he married.

Sometimes a man is embarrassed by the sex act, subconsciously attempting to achieve orgasm as quickly as possible. Other times there may be a problem with overstimulation as a child or a total lack of exposure to sexual stimulation prior to reaching puberty. The specifics are many, but the end result is always premature ejaculation.

Again, all these problems and the others explained in this chapter are easily understood and corrected. They were created by what might be called false self-hypnosis in that an action or idea was focused upon, then reinforced repeatedly until it became an unconscious process affecting your life.

The changes are fairly simple. For example, one self-hypnosis technique will allow you to develop a key word, such as "stop," which you will use when penetrating. You will retain your erection but not orgasm. You will be able to delay your release until after you have satisfied your partner. You enjoy the sensual pleasure of the sex act, the emotional pleasure of not worrying about failing your partner, and the relief of no longer being victimized by premature ejaculation.

There are other techniques as well, each slightly varied according to the cause of the premature ejaculation. But all of them are simple and easy to learn through the use of self-hypnosis.

Women cannot have premature ejaculation but they do have a problem which is equally frustrating during the sex act. This is the inability to get properly aroused for comfortable sex. Often this means an inability to lubricate, resulting in a painful entry by the man, or a tightening of the vaginal muscles which effectively prevents penetration.

Many women try to hide their problem with the faking of sexual pleasure despite the discomfort. Others are able to lubricate but cannot enjoy a release, a situation which makes avoiding telling the partner easier.

Women are further burdened by the same pressures a man faces when he prematurely ejaculates. The woman is not humiliated by the man, but she may greatly frustrate her sexual partner. Some men insist upon knowing whether or not the woman had an orgasm. They feel that they are personally responsible for her happiness and are foolishly insulted if she says no.

Even worse, both men and women may not know what you have learned in the previous chapter concerning the difference between orgasm and climax, each being a natural release following intercourse. Climax is the normal release for many women, as appropriate as orgasm is for others. The difference has to do with their physiology; both types of women enjoy satisfying sex lives. It is only the woman who cannot release who has a problem.

Even knowing all this, the man may be greatly threatened if she does not lie and tell him she achieved orgasm. Thus, she has a tendency to hide the inability to have any release from her partner as long as he can penetrate.

It is important to note that a small number of women do have the equivalent of premature ejaculation. They have an orgasm the instant the man penetrates, then are often aroused to climax again while he is inside. This is certainly not a problem because she is not in pain, she does not disrupt her partner's enjoyment, and she often can find pleasure in the multiple orgasms this situation allows.

The primary reason women who prematurely reach orgasm see a therapist is because they are nervous about what they are feeling during sex. Their physical sensations build more intensely with each release and they think that somehow all this feeling is visible to their partner. They become embarrassed by their natural intensity when, in reality, the male is unaware of what is happening. He is focusing on his own experience during penetration and completely unaware of what she is feeling.

Even during foreplay, kissing and touching, some of these women fear that they will begin to climax or orgasm, a fact they think might show on their face. Again, this is such an internal pleasure that the woman will not reveal these feelings.

The inability to reach climax or orgasm is most common with the emotional sexual woman, though a large number of physical sexual women also fail to achieve release. If you are achieving climax, this is not a problem. It is a natural reaction of the clitoris and fully satisfying for most women who experience it. However, it is not the rolling sensation of orgasm which involves both the clitoris and the vagina. You will later learn how to turn a climax into an orgasm in many cases, but the act of achieving climax is not a problem. It is the inability to release which is a concern.

Many times the reason why lubrication fails to begin is because there is a problem with the fantasy stage of the relationship. This relates to what is known as the message unit concept.

As you recall from Chapter 1, sex is not just a physical act. The mind plays the dominant role in sexual activity. Only after the mind is adequately stimulated through fantasy can there be a physical reaction.

In my work as a therapist with thousands of patients, I have found that each person has a point of overload. This may be one message unit or a hundred or more. Each message unit contains the same psychological thoughts and contributes to the inevitable physiological response.

For example, suppose a man is walking down the street on a windy day. He is the type who finds a woman's legs a sexual stimulant. As he walks, his mind is on business, though he is alert to all that is going on around him. Suddenly a gust of wind catches the skirt of an attractive young woman he is passing, calling attention to her shapely leg. This experience constitutes a sexual message unit to the brain. If the man is both an extreme physical suggestible and an extreme physical sexual as determined in Chapter 2, chances are that he will have an erection at that moment. Other men would simply find the situation pleasurable.

Next the man encounters a billboard advertising a nightclub. There is a photograph of a beautiful woman in tight-fitting clothing, holding a microphone. Her pose is extremely alluring and she seems highly desirable. This is a second message unit bringing the man's mind to male/female relationships and sex.

Then the man rounds a corner and an attractive prostitute is offering her services. She makes an explicit sexual suggestion which he rejects. However, as he continues walking, he thinks about doing the same act with his wife or girl friend. This thought process adds one or more sexual message units to the fantasy stage.

Finally, the man reaches his office and sees that his attractive receptionist is wearing a low-cut blouse and no bra. As he approaches the desk, he is able to look down her blouse. He may think that it would be enjoyable to fondle her breasts or he may think about the breasts of his regular sex partner, again wanting to touch her. More message units related to sex have entered his mind and finally he is overloaded by the sexual stimulation. He has an erection, his body may become slightly warm and flushed, and he wants to go to bed with a woman. He has passed from the fantasy stage to a physical reality stage, even though he has no sexual partner present. He must either masturbate or concentrate on sending enough message units to the brain related to work or some other appropriate interest to lose that erection.

The same is true for women. For example, suppose an executive has been attending male-dominated meetings all day. She has been discussing marketing strategy for new products, the cash flow for the current fiscal year, and other matters, always surrounded by men she finds attractive. Yet not once has she thought sexually, her mind always concentrating on the work at hand.

Finally, there is time for a break. She goes to a restaurant, exhausted from the cares of the day, anxious to have some mental relief, perhaps by reading a novel. The woman takes out a love story and begins reading.

The chapters unfold with a strong female lead, a character the executive finds to be much like herself. The heroine is kidnapped, taken off by a handsome, mysterious stranger, who wants to take her to bed with him. His intentions are obvious and the heroine is properly irate, though he has the sense to be gentle with her.

Gradually the action unfolds, perhaps with a scene in which there is eating and drinking before the moment the heroine has anticipated. Throughout the meal, as they talk and touch, the heroine is finding that her anger has switched to desire. What might have been rape is now rape fantasy, the heroine desiring the slightly forced seduction.

The woman reading this is gradually drawn into it. She fantasizes that the handsome junior executive who made a presentation to her is actually waiting to grab her as she goes to the parking lot. She remembers the way he looked, the smell of his after-shave, and any number of sexual ideas. Each one, including the words in the book, forms message units for her mind.

Then comes the wine she ordered. As she sips the wine, she thinks of a man plying her with alcohol to lower her inhibitions. She notices a man glancing in her direction and fantasizes that he knows of her brains and now, seeing how she looks in person, also desires her body. She is caught up in a fantasy, each message unit reaching the brain until she has experienced enough to have a physical reaction. At that point she lubricates and there is no way to prevent this lubrication.

The reality of sex is that once we reach the overload level of our fantasy stage, and all of us have one, there is no way to prevent lubrication or an erection. It is an action over which we have no conscious control at that time. However, some women do avoid fantasizing and this is frequently where the problem begins. Take the case of Ellen. She is a pharmacist who was complaining because she could not lubricate when she had sex.

> The moment I come home at night, my boy friend is ready to go. He is ready to attack me the instant I close the door, and sometimes carries me to the bedroom, taking off my clothes when we get there. We kiss and touch, and then he can handle no more. He enters me at once, thrusting deeply until he ejaculates. Then he's always concerned that I had as much pleasure as he did, and I usually tell him I did. What he doesn't know is that I don't lubricate and his thrusts are extremely painful.
>
> I don't know if there's something wrong with him or with me. Maybe we should just use Vaseline or something as a lubricant, but that's so messy and I'd feel like only half a woman.

This was an instance where Ellen was an emotional suggestible and her lover was a physical suggestible. She spent all afternoon counting pills and handling prescription problems, never thinking about sex. Her boy friend had been thinking about it for quite some time and was ready to go to bed with her the moment she walked in the door. He used foreplay longer than he felt was necessary in an effort to please Ellen. Yet she never came near to being aroused.

Ellen simply did not have enough message units to be mentally taken through her fantasy stage. She needed to do more thinking about sex before she was with her boy friend so that any extra sexual messages would take her to lubrication. With self-hypnosis, Ellen learned to increase the fantasy stage, adding many more message units before she reached home. Then her boy friend could supply the overload which was so essential for her.

There was nothing wrong with Ellen except for the problem of her fantasy stage. Once that difficulty was resolved through the use of self-hypnosis, lubrication came naturally and quite pleasurably. This is a frequently encountered situation and obviously easily corrected.

Sometimes the reason for the failure to fantasize goes deeper than just an overeager lover who does not understand the mental preparation the woman may require. The woman may have learned as a child that fantasy is somehow bad. Or she may have been told that thinking about sex is wrong. Once she reached adulthood, she felt guilty every time she had normal, healthy fantasies. Thus she found herself denying the use of the essential mechanism for achieving sexual satisfaction. Again, the use of self-hypnosis was able to correct this early, improper conditioning.

This overload concept also explains why some women climax rather than having orgasm. Once the brain is enjoying the fantasy stage of sex, the overload of mental stimulation leads to the physical reaction. She will lubricate and the clitoris will become aroused. Then, either with manual stimulation or penetration, the clitoris is overstimulated, at which time it reaches a climax. This is perfectly natural, though it is not what happens with women who reach orgasm, a reaction involving the vagina as well.

Some women overload the clitoris through stimulation and this, in turn, stimulates the vagina. Then, when the vagina is similarly overloaded during the physical phase of intercourse, the rolling reaction of the orgasm takes place. This is also a normal experience.

Thus it must be understood that some women reach climax because of the way the clitoris handles the stimulation. Other women reach orgasm because both the clitoris and the vagina become involved. Since self-hypnosis trains a woman to control the sensate focus and physical involvement during sex, it is possible for a woman who has enjoyed climax but never experienced orgasm to make the transition. She can learn to transfer the early pleasure of clitoral stimulation to the vaginal area, involving both so that orgasm can be experienced. Orgasm is generally a more intense sensation than clitoral climax, so many women want to learn this approach in order to discover the feeling of such full body involvement. Other women are quite delighted with their climax in the clitoral area. Both are natural.

It is important to remember that while few women are aware of the difference between climax and orgasm, even fewer men have an understanding. The sex partner who is constantly asking his lover whether or not she had an orgasm is actually concerned that she had a release. He is not likely to know that she might have a clitoral climax instead of the vaginal/clitoral orgasm. Thus, it is best early in a relationship you are trying to improve to simply not explain but say that you enjoyed the release. Most men will not press further.

Eventually, you will want to be able to explain to your lover the difference between orgasm and climax if he has not read this book. The reason for this is because you may wish to use self-hypnosis to transfer the sensations and this could take you slightly longer than the normal time for intercourse to which he has become accustomed. If he understands that you have always been satisfied, though your release has been a climax, and that you are seeking to make a good sex life better, he will be more likely to cooperate without being offended.

Note: Never work on improving your sexual relationships with the opposite sex, regardless of whether you are male or female, with the goal being orgasm or release. The constant thought that you must achieve orgasm, that orgasm is the only pleasure in sex, and that without orgasm you are not a man or are less of a woman is extremely self-destructive. Sex is not a physical act whose pleasure comes from orgasm. Sex is a combination of mental and physical stimulation, all of which provide great pleasure.

The sex act starts with the fantasy stage, a pleasant mental experience which is immensely satisfying as a preliminary to touching a special partner. Next comes the enjoyment of bringing in the physical senses of smell, touch, sight, and even sound because the words your partner speaks can be pleasurable and erotic. The movement of the bodies, the caressing, the feelings that come with penetration are all immensely pleasurable. These are what makes sex exciting. They should be physically and mentally savored. You should be concentrating on each stage, leaving yourself open for this total pleasure.

When you approach sex from this viewpoint, everything you experience is delightful and rewarding. You will then naturally overload your mind and body with message units, the release following in a pleasurable manner without your control. But if you concentrate only on this release, you will pay less attention to the message units and will actually risk not developing the natural overload which leads to the release. Your insistence upon thinking only about orgasm actually leads to difficulties achieving the orgasm. This is why self-hypnosis during sex will always concentrate on all the feelings as well as the natural shifting of physical sensations, such as when a woman who climaxes learns to control the clitoral feelings and transfer them to her vagina.

Orgasm is also affected by the law of association. This means that a woman who climaxes can become more sensitive to orgasm by being stimulated in more than one area at the same time. The more areas giving her pleasure through stimulation as she approaches climax, the more likely she is to develop the outward ripple effect that is orgasm. Again, this combination of physical and mental stimulation to build an even better sex life is most easily achieved through the controlled thought process that is self-hypnosis.

As a woman becomes aware of the timing for climax, she is able to work towards orgasm with her partner. Both the clitoris and the vagina are swollen during the sex act. Many women are able to learn to sense when they are about to climax, backing off slightly from a cooperating partner so that there is stimulation given to the vagina. This only takes a few seconds, but it is enough time to transfer the feelings to involve the vagina. After this is accomplished, orgasm is likely to occur, if not the first time you do it, certainly with a little practice.

It may be necessary to experiment with sexual positions and forms of stimulation during this time. The clitoral area for a woman will vary. Some women have a high clitoral area and others have a low clitoral area. The high clitoral area may require manual stimulation to be effective, the position being such that a man's penis may not be able to be inserted at an effective angle. The low clitoral area is much easier for the penis to reach and the stimulation can be improved for the woman just by experimenting with position, often by having the woman on top. When there is difficulty, some combination of manual stimulation, oral stimulation, and penetration will allow for adequate mental overload to achieve orgasm. Again, remember that it is the enjoyment of the full sex act, not just the goal of orgasm, which leads to maximum results.

It is also important to remember that climax is a natural end to the sex act for some women. While many women who climax can learn to have an orgasm, others will always climax and this is fine. Should you climax and want to learn to have an orgasm, by all means experiment with the information found later in this book. However, if you find that you increase your enjoyment of the sex act but always end with a climax, this is not a problem. You are someone who will always climax and this is as proper a release as any woman who may also have an orgasm.

Inability to Climax

"I'm not having the problems you describe, Dr. Kappas," said Janeen, a publicist for an entertainment company.

> I can fantasize about sex and really get turned on. I've been known to read a sexy novel on my lunch break and become so flushed some of the other women tease me about it.
>
> When my husband and I are together, we talk freely about sex and his touch turns me on almost instantly. I'm lubricated and sometimes feel he can't penetrate me fast enough. I want him, I want to enjoy him, yet nothing happens. I'm moist and ready, yet there is no release.
>
> I used to climax all the time when we were living together. But now that we got married, I can't seem to enjoy sex with him the same way. Everything is right, from my desire to my ability to lubricate, but no matter what position we use or how long he holds back his orgasm, I can't seem to climax.

Janeen and I talked about her background. She lived with Arthur, her husband, for almost three years before they got married. They traveled together and were quite open about their relationship. She continued:

> I didn't want the commitment of marriage at first. My parents have been married fifty years. They got married right out of high school, saved for their own home, had a bunch of kids, and did everything right. The only thing they didn't do was love each other. By the time I was born, they were like two strangers stuck in a relationship neither wanted. They had sex, they went places together, but they also led separate lives. I think they would have divorced years ago if they hadn't felt that there was a taboo to that sort of thing.
>
> All the time I was growing up they would always talk about how marriage was forever. They really believed that "for better or worse" nonsense. I can see them staying together when finances go bad or when one of them becomes seriously ill, but when the love stopped and they stayed together because it was "right," that just caused a lot of pain.

Arthur and I were determined not to make the same mistake my parents did. We wanted to see how we related after a year or two. We realized the intense physical passion of the new relationship could diminish. We knew we could begin leading separate lives in the same house. That's why we decided to avoid the commitment, even though my parents were irate. They told me that I shouldn't be living in sin. They carried on terribly about the disgrace, even though some of their friends had retired to Florida, been widowed, and were living with someone to increase their Social Security checks instead of remarrying. It was awful the way they talked to us until we finally married, though at least we waited until the time was right for us.

Janeen didn't realize this until after we had talked, but her problem was a typical one. She was unable to release because she was punishing herself. She had felt guilt from what her parents told her over the years, as well as when she began living with Arthur. Subconsciously, she felt she was doing something wrong because of the way her parents had programmed her over the years. She did not realize this, but it was the cause of her inability to climax despite a normal sex drive with healthy desire.

Guilt can take other forms in this situation as well. There can be guilt because of religious training, peer group pressure, an old belief system which has changed only on the conscious level, and numerous other ways. It is only by understanding this fact, using self-hypnosis to reprogram your subconscious mind, that this is changed.

Parents frequently stress sex as a taboo subject during adolescence. Even the best of parents become somewhat fearful that their children will engage in sexual activity which might result in pregnancy or disease. The parents do not discuss the pleasure of sex and the naturalness of extreme desire. They do not try to give adequate information so that if a child experiments with sex against the parents' will, at least the child will do it with an understanding of the need to take precautions. Instead, they give so many warnings that the child may even feel dirty by having normal sexual arousal and/or by seeking relief through masturbation.

Many children rebel against the parents' attitudes, coming to the conclusion that responsible sex is fine. They may indulge in sex before marriage and find it quite enjoyable. Yet subconsciously their minds often rebel, trying to find some way to punish themselves for doing what they learned was taboo. Unless they recognize this fact and work this mature understanding through to the subconscious mind, they can be victimized by their early teachings. This may occur years after the child has left home and engaged in adult activity.

Sometimes embarrassment can prevent the release for a woman. Some girls do not like their appearance or feel that something is wrong. Most teenagers of both sexes are constantly concerned with whether or not they are appealing to the opposite sex. They may become envious of some boy or girl whom they feel represents everything they are not. This also adds to that feeling of physical inferiority.

All of this can lead to the adult worrying about what will happen when the sex partner sees them as they really are. They may want sex only in the dark, be ashamed to undress in front of the partner, or otherwise be embarrassed. This constant feeling can undermine the sex act, preventing the natural enjoyment which would otherwise be present.

There is also a performance problem. Someone having sex for the first time, especially a woman, may fear that a more experienced partner will not find him or her appealing. There is a belief that the other person may become bored or not have a good time because of this lack of experience. Instead of letting go and exploring the relationship in any way which comes naturally, the person is tense and unable to reach climax, even when some of the early stages of the sex act take place. Again, the use of self-hypnosis can break down the extreme inhibitions which develop.

Some men and women have great difficulty fantasizing. They may be able to describe emotional feelings but be unable to describe physical feelings. Or they may be able to describe physical sensations and not be comfortable talking about emotions. It is literally impossible, without changing themselves through self-hypnosis or counseling, to experience adequate fantasy to have sex.

Often their inability to fantasize comes from a background in which they were taught that fantasy was wrong. Some religious groups feel that a sexual fantasy about someone is as sinful as having sex with the person. All of us are aroused by others. This begins with puberty and usually carries through all our lives. Sometimes it is someone with whom we develop a physical relationship. Other times it is someone we view from afar. This is a normal part of being human, yet there are groups that teach that such fantasies are adulterous or otherwise evil. Teenagers feel guilty for their urges and, as adults, they have forced themselves to cease fantasizing. Without fantasy, there can be no physical arousal.

Some people do not have religious taboos in their backgrounds yet also have trouble with fantasy. A few individuals are extremely literal-minded. These are people who take life exactly as it comes. When they have an apple, an orange, and a banana, they may look at them and wonder how they can fairly divide them among three different people since each piece of fruit is different. The individual who can fantasize will see these three pieces of fruit and decide to make a fruit salad so that everyone shares equally.

The individual who is unable to fantasize is usually the extremely emotional sexual who is also an extreme emotional suggestible, a fairly uncommon combination. Should you fall into this minority, you can change yourself through practicing fantasy while in self-hypnosis. Change is relatively slow, yet it can be done.

Other Problems

For some men and women, the needs of their sex partner can act as a turn-off. One person needs to verbalize the sexual experience. He or she wants to talk about the sex act, what he or she is feeling, what he or she is doing, and/or be extremely descriptive of what he or she would like to do. Such an individual becomes sexually aroused with such talk. It may be necessary for part of the fantasy prior to experiencing the physical changes of erection or lubrication. The problem comes with the partner who may find that talk of sex is a turn-off.

Often the person who has trouble becoming physically aroused or maintaining that arousal when the partner is talking about sex is someone who has been raised to think that sex talk is dirty. A nice person doesn't say such things and you should only have a relationship with a nice person. Again, there is a need to desensitize to past conditioning in order to fully enjoy sex without inhibiting the partner's needs.

Perhaps the greatest turn-off to sex experienced by some men and women is when the woman has continual vaginal infections. There are certain types of vaginal infections which doctors unfamiliar with aspects of the sexual experience have been unable to solve. They supply medication and warn the woman about sexual problems during the time when the infection is at its worst, but they cannot keep the infection from returning.

The reason such difficulties persist may be from physical problems which are correctable. It is only with the problem routinely called the Honeymoon Disease that self-hypnosis, not medicine, is the long-term solution to preventing a recurrence.

The reason the problem is called the Honeymoon Disease is because it is caused by frequent lubrication without sexual release. It is often during the honeymoon that sex is on the minds of the couple more than any other activity. The woman may lubricate with great frequency during the day and night, having sex less often than mental desire creates a physical reaction. The lubrication lying dormant will cause infection when the air strikes the area.

The strong physical sexual woman who is a high emotional suggestible is the most likely individual to experience the Honeymoon Disease problem. She has a strong sex drive and is frequently thinking about sex. Books she reads, men she sees, relationships she experiences vicariously while watching television will all trigger the sex drive. She will become mentally stimulated enough to have the overload which leads to the physical reaction of lubrication. This occurs when either she is not with a sex partner or when it is inappropriate to have sex.

Such an individual may lubricate several times a day, yet may have sex only once a day, if at all. The condition is especially upsetting for the woman without a relationship at the moment so that there is no chance to clear the lubrication through the normal process of intercourse. Thus there is always a surface available to be infected by the chemical process created when air strikes the lubricated area.

There are two possible answers to this problem. For some women, it is as simple as increasing their sexual activity. A woman with an ongoing relationship and a readily available sex partner may find that a slight increase in sexual activity rechannels her thought process so that the mental arousal occurs only when intercourse can take place.

Other women are not so fortunate. They are not in a position to increase their sexual activity or they may find that they lubricate more frequently than can be controlled with an increase in activity. For such individuals, self-hypnosis provides a method for reducing the fantasy stage. The women learn to mentally stimulate themselves less frequently, reducing the lubrication, and giving the infection a chance to heal. They can still utilize fantasy to thoroughly enjoy sex, but they reduce the amount of fantasy during inappropriate times, preventing the degree of lubrication that was causing a problem.

Some women have a tendency to tighten the vaginal muscles and prevent penetration. This is the result of an unconscious control from past experience.

These past experiences can be many. Some women fear pregnancy, regardless of what precautions they may be taking. This fear builds up until their unconscious mind takes over during the sexual fantasy stage. They then tighten the muscles at the time of penetration.

The extreme physical sexual who has been rejected by a previous lover in a way that left her deeply hurt will have trouble becoming aroused by a new partner. She is so unconsciously afraid of being hurt again that she will tighten the muscles to protect herself from sex she actually desires. If he cannot penetrate, he cannot hurt her emotionally the way the previous partner was able to. The fact that she truly desires this new partner will not stop the control until she fully deals with the past hurt and is able to prevent it from maintaining this control.

There can also be great anger towards men because of past hurt. Sometimes this occurs when a partner rejected the woman and she wants to hurt the new man by denying him the control of the previous lover. Other times the anger may stem from abuse as a child, rape, or some other extremely bad experience.

The anger is not logical. The man who suffers in the positive relationship is not the same as the one who came before. The woman who is having this trouble with such a partner has not been able to view the new relationship for what it is. She needs to utilize self-hypnosis so that she can transfer the anger from that portion of her brain which simply reacts to a situation, moving it to the portion of her brain where she has logical reasoning. Once the problem is transferred in this way, the woman is able to view the past and present in perspective, moving forward with her relationship.

Other Male Problems

Premature ejaculation is the primary problem faced by a man having difficulty with sex. The opposite situation, retarded ejaculation where he cannot get a release, is a difficulty that is also reported with great frequency.

There are two forms of retarded ejaculation. The more common involves the man who cannot get a release. The other occurs when the man can release but it takes so long that the woman becomes numb, sore, and bored. Both are frustrated and what started as a pleasurable act has suddenly become an endurance problem for both of them. It is extremely frustrating for the man and unpleasant for the woman.

Performance anxiety is a common problem, although the reasons behind such difficulties will vary. Both men and women suffer such concerns, sometimes because of past humiliation and other times for less obvious reasons. A child caught masturbating may be humiliated about the sex act. He or she may feel that sex is dirty and be afraid to engage in it. This fear then dominates the subconscious as an adult and performance anxiety affects what would otherwise be a positive relationship.

Not all the sexual problems I encounter as a therapist are serious. I once had an emotional sexual male come to me complaining of being impotent. I questioned him extensively and learned that he regularly had orgasm and had no problem becoming aroused. However, he was convinced that he was impotent and his fear had been confirmed by a sex therapist.

Closer questioning revealed that the man often lasted thirty minutes before orgasming, a time long enough to bring a woman to orgasm at least once and often several times. I probed deeper and discovered that he was married to an extreme physical sexual who liked to go an hour or longer in marathon sex sessions. Her demands were actually excessive and her husband certainly had no problems with impotency. And the sex therapist who had made the diagnosis? His wife!

I must admit at this point that there are some problems that were solved, not through the self-hypnosis you will learn in the next chapter, but by circumstances of a more unusual nature. My favorite incident occurred when a tall, muscular, handsome man frantically demanded an appointment to see me. The man explained he had a sex problem and his voice indicated that he was almost hysterical about his trouble.

You've got to help me! I'm in serious trouble. I can't have an erection. I've tried and tried with my girl friend but I just can't have an erection. I had one all the time in the past, but suddenly I'm in trouble. You've got to see me as fast as possible.

The man was so desperate, that I agreed to see him on a Saturday at a time when I normally would not come into the office. I knew that no matter what the cause, the emotional reaction to such failure is so devastating that I could not let him suffer. However, he never came in to see me. Instead he called my secretary, elated with the change.

"I can get an erection!" he exclaimed. "I won't need to see Dr. Kappas after all. I can get an erection!"

Naturally my secretary was pleased. She then asked him how he did it. "It was easier than I thought," he said. "I just got a new girl friend."

More serious is the fear of intimacy which affects both men and women, though more often women. Usually this comes from a past love affair which ended in a way that was unexpected.

Sex is far more casual today than it was in the past. Sex is often enjoyed for itself in a relationship between friends who may never become long-term intimates. However, should one of the partners equate sex and love, this can result in a serious problem. This partner, frequently the woman, will plan her entire future around the other person. The act of sex constantly reinforces the belief that there is a deep love between them, even though the other person does not feel the same way. Each partner has blinders when it comes to fully recognizing the views of the other.

Then the relationship ends, the couple drifting apart. The one partner feels no strong emotions, having enjoyed the relationship while it was intense, then accepting the fact that it was never intense enough to last.

The other partner is deeply hurt and angry. He or she was greatly in love. The sex act was proof of this love and should not have been taken so casually. The fact that this is often not the first sex partner, nor was this someone who saved his or her virginity until the perfect mate came along, is not considered. All that matters is that the person gave his/her heart and was then spurned. There is both great anger and a fear of being hurt.

Sometimes the partner from such a relationship also has problems. This person has felt so smothered by the possessiveness of the previous lover that he or she is afraid to commit to anyone else. He or she cannot function in the new relationship for fear that the experience of the past would repeat itself.

Often the self-hypnosis techniques needed to correct such problems are quite simple. Usually, they involve visualizing a sense of competence and security in the relationship. The man or woman learns to feel confidence which had been shattered by the problems which seemed so overwhelming before.

Another common cause of problems comes with the man or woman who has had casual sex in the past and then meets the person he or she thinks is the perfect partner. Suddenly all the fantasy of sex becomes a reality. This is the person with whom the individual wants to spend a lifetime. There is romance, the emotions of the first time, and the individual wants to feel as though the relationship is unique.

In this circumstance, the person who is feeling this way, usually the woman, will want to be virginal. Suddenly there is guilt over the sexual relationships of the past. The fact that the past relationships were enjoyable and perfectly all right at the time means nothing. They are suddenly dirty because the person feels they should never have happened. Only now is the relationship perfect, and the individual damaged the present with the past actions.

The result of these emotions is a subconscious rejection of sex. There is an inability to have an orgasm, failure to lubricate, a tightening of muscles, and other problems. These are all meant to act as punishment, even though there is no reason for this self-punishment. Thus there is a need to understand the past and desensitize the problems. The woman or man involved learns to view the current relationship logically under self-hypnosis.

Obviously the variety of problems which you can have are many, yet the causes are always quite simple. Sex can be and should be one of the most enjoyable of all human experiences. By using the self-hypnosis techniques you will learn in the next chapters, you will be able to experience the immense pleasure and variety of experiences you have always desired.

Self-hypnosis

5

The use of self-hypnosis and sex is a natural relationship which is extremely easy to learn. You can deliberately place yourself in this state at any time you desire during the sex act. However, in order to have this facility, you will need to practice self-hypnosis in advance. This practice should be started as soon as possible, repeating it for a few minutes each day until it becomes second nature for you. In addition to mastering this natural function of the human mind, you will also find it extremely relaxing.

The Relaxation Phase

Place yourself in a semi-comfortable position. This may mean sitting upright on a comfortable chair or propped up on pillows in bed. You should select an approach which is not likely to put you to sleep. You will be extremely relaxed and can easily drift off to sleep. There is nothing wrong with doing this, but you will need to stay awake during the self-hypnotic induction if you are to learn this skill.

You want to remain aware, to be able to formulate suggestions. A completely comfortable position, such as lying flat on the bed, will most likely cause you to go to sleep. If you must stay on the bed, keep your head propped at least twelve inches above the level of your feet.

In either instance, take off your shoes so that you have air circulating around your feet. This will make you more sensitive since there will be no constricting of a part of your body.

Now make yourself sensitive to your body. Move your body until you do not feel restricted by your clothing or any other physical discomforts. Think of yourself as floating free, unhampered in any way.

Once you are comfortable, think of your hands. This is the area where the greatest change in skin resistance takes place. Just by concentrating on your hands, you will feel some physiological changes taking place.

To demonstrate this to yourself as you are sitting comfortably, stare at your hands. Attempt to feel some tingling sensation or numbness, almost as if whatever is inside of the skin is expanding and trying to get out of it.

Now take your hand and place it back on your chair, continuing to be aware of this sensation or feeling. Does your hand feel cold or numb? Is it feeling overly relaxed? Is it heavy? Is it relaxed? Pick one word that best describes what you are feeling and try to correlate the feeling with the word.

Concentrate on your hand for approximately three to five minutes. When you sense the feeling growing stronger, say the word to yourself. For example, you might say, "I am feeling a cold, tingling sensation…a tingling, cold sensation."

Now take the words "cold" and "tingling" and try to decide which one you are feeling the most. Whichever word you select will become your physical key word. Of course, this can be any word which relates. I am using "cold" and "tingling" for my example.

Once you have established your physical key, gently lay your hands across the top of your legs. Each time you think of that physical key word, you will think of that sensation.

Concentrate on the rest of your body, moving your attention to your arms, your shoulders, your thighs, and so forth, on to the bottoms of your feet. Each time you think of a new location, mention the key word and try to recall the same feeling that you had in your hands. In our example, you might think "cold" when concentrating on your ankles and the other parts of your body.

Once the physical key word sensation is achieved and controlled, the law of association becomes extremely strong. This means that when you say the word, you also sense the feeling which led you to select it originally. This fact will help you with the rest of the self-hypnosis conditioning process which involves your emotional and intellectual keys.

As the physiological change takes place (you think "cold" while concentrating on a part of your body and you sense coldness there, for example), and your mind associates it with your physical key word, the psychological effect will begin to take place. The fact that you are controlling one aspect of your physical body allows your emotions to run free and leads to your second or emotional key.

At this point you will say to yourself, "The tingling sensation causes relaxation moving into my toes, into my heels, my ankles, and into the calves of my legs. I become aware of my legs pushing down and this tingling sensation moving back up into my thighs and my hips. I am aware of the contact between my hands and my thighs, and this tingling sensation will soon move upward into my arms. As I become aware of my stomach muscles relaxing, I become aware of this tingling sensation moving upward and I become aware of my breathing."

Since your breathing reflects a stronger effect on emotional change than any other function of your body, this area should be used to establish and trigger your emotional key. Concentrate on your breathing until you feel it beginning to expand. Then try to become aware of your emotional feeling and attempt to tie in some positive word that can affect your emotional feelings at this moment. This will increase the strong effect of the law of association.

Keep in mind that you do not want to have any negative feelings or emotions. You should use only positive words such as "happiness," "success," "confidence," "peacefulness" or whatever other word gives you a sensation of elation or well-being. Each time you say the words, pause and try to become aware of any emotion you feel For example, if the word is "happy," you will tie in this word with the physical sensation of your breathing and the drawing of new oxygen into the blood. Should this be the word you select, then "happy" will become your emotional key.

Finally, you will need the intellectual key. This is the third and most important of the key words for self-hypnosis. However, this word will be the same for everyone. You will either use "deep hypnotic sleep" or just "deep sleep."

Sleep is a basic human need. It is a condition to which we have been responding from the day we are born. We yield to this condition each night, allowing our minds to become still and go almost blank for a few moments before drifting into the normal escape mechanism called sleep.

Your subconscious mind can only relate to a condition of behavior. Thus each time you place yourself in this position, your subconscious mind assumes that you are going to sleep and your conscious mind is allowed to go into unconsciousness, drifting into a normal sleep.

During this period, your body is allowed to rest. More important, through dreams, your mind is allowed to vent all the thoughts, traumas, ideas, and events that no longer have any value to you. Sleep then becomes an extremely strong intellectual conditioning. You cannot deny the fact that you can, will, and must sleep. Your intellectual suggestibility, which requires logic and reason, must respond to the suggestion of "deep sleep."

You will utilize this condition in self-hypnosis. However, you will alter a few of the factors which would normally put you to sleep in order to remain open to suggestion.

First, change the position of your body so that it is different from the position you would normally assume for sleep. This is why I suggested avoiding the bed or, if you must be in bed, keeping your head elevated at least twelve inches above your legs so that its level is different from that you would use for sleep.

Second, you will either say "deep hypnotic sleep" or just "deep sleep" since the word "deep" is one not normally used when at rest. This will help further distinguish between the two states.

In the beginning, the techniques described may place you only in a very light hypnotic state. With repetition, the suggestions will become more natural, the state of hypnosis will deepen, and you will feel a very strong response to the three key words.

Any stimulus played over and over in the mind soon becomes a habit or trigger mechanism. Experiments have been conducted in the creation of automatic trigger mechanisms to see how frequently a suggestion must be repeated and practiced before it is a part of the subconscious. We have discovered that with twenty-one repetitions under hypnosis, any condition placed properly in the mind becomes a trigger mechanism with ever growing strength.

During your early practice sessions, you may find yourself experiencing the preliminary aspects of sleep. You may start to sense the rapid eye movement of the dream state or even have your eyes start to roll up under the eyelids. You should encourage this condition by letting your eyes roll up, at the same time repeating the words "deep hypnotic sleep." This will develop the natural law of association between the rolling of the eyes and the words "deep hypnotic sleep."

There are many myths about hypnosis. One of these is that you are giving up all control and conscious awareness when you are hypnotized, by yourself or others. The truth is quite different, though. Thus you may be surprised to find that you have full conscious awareness when you have entered this hypnotic state. Do not be concerned. The natural state of self-hypnosis always retains full conscious awareness. This is your clue to the fact that you are in the hypnotic state rather than the normal sleep state.

On television and in novels, someone who is hypnotized seems to drop into a deep, black whirlpool or perhaps experience some dramatic sounds. Bells may ring, lightning flashes, and the world seems to somehow change. Yet none of this occurs in reality. It is a natural condition over which you have full control and does not result in such sound and fury.

While in self-hypnosis, you will hear everything around you. You will have full conscious awareness, though you will feel a little as you do when awake and daydreaming. You will be relaxed and feel slightly detached from those all around. Your mind may wander, you may feel a numbness or tingling in your fingers and toes, and/or you may feel somewhat dissociated from those all around.

You may also forget the subject on which you wanted to concentrate. This is no problem. In such a relaxed state, it is natural for your mind to wander. The important step is for you to learn the self-hypnosis and to practice until the condition becomes automatic.

Self-Hypnosis Conditioning: Summary

Assuming that your key words are "tingling," "happy," and "deep hypnotic sleep," you will place yourself in a semi-comfortable position. Your hands will be resting on your thighs. As you concentrate on your hands, you will feel a tingling sensation in your hands. The tingling sensation will move down your body and into your legs. Once it reaches your feet, you will then reverse the action, suggesting that you will feel this tingling sensation into your toes, your heels, your ankles, the calves of your legs, moving upward to the area where there is contact between your hands and your legs, and then upwards through your midsection.

As this relaxation begins to move upwards into your stomach muscles and solar plexus, you become aware that it continues up through your arms. At this point you will concentrate upward to your breathing and place all your attention on your breathing. As this happens, say your emotional key word silently to yourself. In our example, the word is "happy," and it will begin to represent the condition of your emotional state.

Continue to be aware of your breathing as the relaxation continues to move through your shoulders, up your back, into your neck muscles, through your scalp, and across your forehead. As it begins to move down through your facial muscles and jaw muscles, you become aware that your eyes have a tendency to roll upwards under the lids.

As you recognize this upward movement of the eyes, plant the words "deep hypnotic sleep" over and over in your mind. This will strengthen the natural law of association.

The Awakening Procedure

Before going any further, it is important to become aware of the awakening procedure. This involves a series of steps you will use to bring yourself out of the hypnotic state. It is a very important part of any hypnotic suggestion.

The awakening procedure is meant to create a condition in which you are brought fully out of the hypnotic state. Without this procedure, you will remain for a period of time in a highly suggestible state. You will be suggestible not only to your own thoughts but to the stimuli all around. This means that if any negative ideas are presented, you might let these have great power over your actions. Since you are learning self-hypnosis in order to have more positive personal and sexual relations, you want to be certain to avoid any chance of increasing negative ideas.

The awakening procedure involves creating a condition which your mind will associate with awakening. The best procedure is to count from zero through five (zero, one, two, three, four, five) and say the words "wide awake." After you have placed yourself in a hypnotic state a few times, then brought yourself out of it, you will begin to recognize the feelings associated with each state. This will probably not occur at first as you are learning, but be assured that both stages are occurring.

When entering the state of hypnosis, some people have what they report as a twinge of current passing over their forehead. Others say that they have a sense of numbness or a sense of calm. Whatever you experience, and it may be quite different from these states, there will be a definite reaction which you can sense.

There is also a change upon awakening. This may be a slight trembling or a renewed alertness. Again, each person is likely to be somewhat different, but everyone feels something specific. These feelings are important because you will always be aware of when you are in or out of self-hypnosis.

While you are learning self-hypnosis to help your sex life, you will want to practice daily. This practice should be deliberate and separate from your sexual relations. You may want to use the condition to prepare yourself for sex, giving yourself whatever suggestions are appropriate for your desires, but it should be attempted regardless of how you do it. Ideally this will also mean spending at least fifteen minutes each day in the self-hypnotic condition.

There is a chance that you will be disturbed during your practice. Ideally you will learn self-hypnosis while alone at home or some other quiet location. But even under the best of circumstances, the telephone might ring, there may be a knock at the door or, if you are outside, someone may pass. The moment you are disturbed, be certain to count yourself out (zero, one, two, three, four, five, wide awake). Just because your eyes are open, you are walking around, and you are aware of all that is going on, this does not mean that you are out of the hypnotic state. You are actually continuing to be open to both positive and negative suggestions from your own thoughts and the statements of those around you. This is especially bad when you consider the fact that there are more negatives on the news, in newspapers, and in everyday life than positive suggestions, thus giving you the risk of creating anxiety and mild depression.

If you notice these symptoms and remember that you had not taken yourself out of hypnosis, you can easily correct this problem. Go through the procedure for entering self-hypnosis, then count yourself out, being certain to end with the words "wide awake."

The degree of hyper-suggestibility you can develop will vary with the individual. Some men and women report that they are quite skilled after a day and are able to apply it easily to their sex lives almost immediately. Others take a week and still others may take months to truly be able to work quickly on entering. However, right from the start, everyone is able to begin changing their subconscious. This complete mastery, which may take many weeks for some, is *not* a factor in your ability to improve and intensify your sexual relations. Once you are able to enter the self-hypnotic state, and you will do that the first time you try the approach outlined, you will begin improving your sex life. You will be able to correct any problems which might exist and make your current sex life, if pleasurable, even greater than you had once thought possible.

A Self-Hypnosis Induction

Now that you understand how to induce self-hypnosis, this section will show you how you will talk yourself through the hypnotic state. In the next chapter, you will learn to apply the hypnosis so that you can radically improve your sex life, no matter how delightful it may be already.

Start by placing yourself in a semi-comfortable position as described. Have your shoes off and move about until you feel that you are unencumbered and free. Your hands should be resting on your thighs, your eyes closed, your mind drifting over your entire body.

Concentrate on your hands. Say your physical key word and allow yourself to feel the change taking place. Now say:

I begin to feel this sense of physical relaxation moving from my hands, into my thighs, going down through my knees into the calves of my leg... moving down into my ankles, to my feet, right up to my toes, relaxing the feet completely.

Now I concentrate on this relaxation at the tip of my toes, moving down towards my heels, up to my ankles, through the calves of my legs, up to my knees. And I feel the sensation of relaxation moving through my thighs, through my hips, all the way up to my waist, relaxing the entire lower half of my body now.

I concentrate on my stomach muscles relaxing. I feel that I am letting go, allowing them to become very loose, very limp, just letting go. I concentrate on this relaxation moving up to my chest area, and I become aware of my breathing.

Now inhale and say your emotional key word to yourself. Feel this emotional change take place.

I concentrate on this relaxation moving under my arms, going up in my back, encasing my entire back. I feel my back pressing down as I relax, and I allow this relaxation to move up, into my shoulders. My shoulders become very limp and loose, just like a rag doll, relaxing.

I concentrate on this relaxation, moving from my shoulders, into my neck, relaxing all my muscles, relaxing every fiber, every nerve and tissue in my neck, completely relaxing them now. I concentrate on this relaxation moving up into my head area, relaxing my entire head.

First I relax all my facial muscles, my jaw muscles, and I allow the slight separation of my lips and I feel a slight dryness. The urge to swallow is taking place. (This is very normal with self-hypnosis.)

I concentrate on this relaxation moving up into my eyelids, and my eyes have a tendency to roll up under my eyelids.

At this point you say your intellectual key word to yourself.

I concentrate on this relaxation moving into my scalp, my forehead relaxing, allowing the blood to circulate very freely, very close to the skin now. With every breath, I exhale.

I go deeper into relaxation now. Deeper. Deeper. And with every breath I inhale, I welcome this relaxation. And as I exhale, I let go, going deeper and deeper into hypnosis, enjoying every moment now, enjoying every second as I go deeper and deeper.

I begin to feel this inner peace, this inner calmness, and I like this feeling. And I'm going to allow this inner calmness to carry over into my daily life and become part of my life.

Now repeat your three key words to yourself and say, "Each time I say these words, I will sleep soundly and deeply. Each time I will go deeper than the time before."

Now imagine yourself standing at the top of a staircase, looking down twenty steps.

As I count from twenty down to zero, each number will represent a step taking me deeper into relaxation, deeper into self-hypnosis.

Now I begin going down. Twenty, nineteen, eighteen, seventeen, sixteen, fifteen, fourteen, deeper and deeper, now. Thirteen, twelve, eleven, ten, nine, eight, deeper and deeper now, seven, six, five, four, three, two, one. Deeper asleep now. Deeper. Deeper.

Now that I am learning to control this state of self-hypnosis, I begin to feel that I have a definite advantage over most people. I have access to my subconscious mind, the most powerful part of my mind. I can feel and be only the way I want to feel and be.

And I can also now suggest to myself that I will accept only positive thoughts and ideas which are beneficial to me for my well-being and self-improvement. I have the ability to reject all negative thoughts, ideas, suggestions, or inferences from anyone, and I am developing more control over my mind and body.

Each and every time I encounter a situation where, in the past, I became tense, nervous, upset, or fearful, I will find now that I am more relaxed, calmer, more confident, more sure of myself. I have the ability to handle situations so much better than ever before.

Now, in a few moments, I am going to awaken myself. I am going to count from zero to five, and when I reach five, I will open my eyes and I will awaken completely and totally. Physically, I will feel very relaxed; emotionally, very calm, very peaceful, and very happy. Mentally, I will feel very sharp, very alert, thinking very clearly. And then I will place myself in the hypnotic state again, strengthening my conditioning, going into self-hypnosis.

Zero, one, two, slowly and gently coming up now. Three, feeling more refreshed, more relaxed, feeling like I have had hours of restful sleep. Four, and four becomes a very alert number to me. I begin to feel my breathing changing, the movement in my eyes taking place. Almost awake now. Five. I'm wide awake. Wide awake now. Wide awake.

Now that I'm in a semi-comfortable position, my hands on my thighs, I concentrate on my physical key word, saying it to myself. I am feeling this physical sensation of relaxation moving from my hands, to my thighs, moving down into my knees, the calves of my legs, relaxing the calves of my legs completely.

I am feeling the weight of my legs pressing down now. As this relaxation moves down into my ankles, into my feet, down into my heels, and then moving into my toes, my feet relax completely. I concentrate on this relaxation, reversing from my toes, moving through my heels, up through my ankles, moving through the calves of my legs, relaxing every muscle, every nerve, every fiber, every tissue in my leg, allowing the blood to circulate very freely. It is very close to the skin, unrestricted, as all of the muscles and nerves relax.

This sensation of relaxation moves through my knees, and in through my thighs, in through my hips, all the way up to my waist and midsection. I concentrate on my stomach muscles relaxing. With every breath I exhale, I feel the muscles letting go, relaxing them very deeply.

This concentration of relaxation now moves up into the chest muscles and I become aware of my breathing. I become aware of every time I inhale and every time I exhale. I feel the movements of my body as I inhale and exhale.

And as I inhale, I say my emotional key word to myself (say the word), implanting that word very deeply into my mind. And I allow the sensation of relaxation to move up into my shoulders, allowing them to feel very limp, loose, just like a rag doll.

I feel the weight of my arms and I become aware of how my arms are hinged to my shoulders. And then my shoulders relax. I allow my arms to relax, feeling the weight of my arms pressing down.

I concentrate on this relaxation moving down from my shoulders, down into my back. I relax my entire back now, relaxing it completely. This relaxation moves into my neck and I relax every fiber, every muscle, every nerve and tissue in my neck. Deeply relaxing my neck.

I feel this relaxation moving up into my head, starting with my jaw and jaw muscles. I allow my jaw to relax completely until I feel a slight parting of my lips. A dryness takes place on my lips and soon the urge to swallow will follow.

And then I concentrate on all my facial muscles relaxing together now. This relaxation moves up to my eyes and my eyelids. As I begin to relax my eyelids, I begin to sense my eyes have a tendency to roll upward. And as this takes place, I say (use your last key word) and I go deep, deep asleep.

This relaxation works up into my forehead and I allow this relaxation to move into my scalp, relaxing all my scalp muscles, allowing the blood to circulate and move freely, very close to the skin.

I am relaxing my entire head now, and as the relaxation invades my entire body, from my toes all the way up to my head, and from my head all the way down to my toes, I feel like a peaceful, pleasant blanket of relaxation has passed over me. And with every breath I exhale, I continue to go deeper and deeper into hypnosis, deeper into relaxation. I begin to feel the positive sensation of relaxation in my entire being. I begin to welcome this relaxation with every breath I inhale. And as I exhale, I allow myself to go deeper and deeper. Deeper and deeper.

In a few moments, I am going to take myself deeper into this state. I begin to imagine myself standing at the top of a staircase, looking down. Each number represents another step, going deeper and deeper into hypnosis, deeper and deeper into relaxation. And when I reach zero, I will be deeper than ever before.

Now I begin going down. Twenty, nineteen, eighteen, seventeen, sixteen, fifteen, fourteen, thirteen, twelve, eleven, ten, deeper and deeper now. Nine, eight, seven, six, going down. Five, four, three, going all the way down. Two, one, zero, and deeper asleep, now. Deeper and deeper.

Now I allow my mind to drift over my entire body, and I feel this relaxation becoming more prominent. I am enjoying every moment now, as I go deeper and deeper, knowing I am gaining more and more control over my mind and body. I have access to the most powerful part of my mind, my subconscious, so I can choose the ways *I* want to feel, so I can become the way *I* want to become. I know that my mind is receptive to positive thoughts, ideas, and directions which give me a feeling of the way *I* want to become. I know that my mind is receptive to positive thoughts, ideas, and directions which give me a feeling of well-being. And each time I use my formula and desire to enter this state, I go in quickly, soundly, and deeply.

Each time I will go deeper than the time before, knowing that this condition becomes stronger with each passing day.

In a few moments, I am going to suggest to myself that I will accept only positive thoughts and ideas that are beneficial to me for my well-being, for my self-improvement. I will have the ability to reject all negative thoughts, ideas, or inferences from anyone. And each time I approach a situation where, in the past, I became nervous, tense, upset, or fearful, I will find now I am more relaxed, calmer, more confident, and more sure of myself. And I begin to like myself more.

And now as I become aware of this peacefulness and this calmness, I find I like this feeling. I like this feeling so much, I am going to hold on to this feeling. Nothing and no one will take this feeling from me, because it belongs to me. This control over my mind and body belongs to me.

And now I am going to imagine I am watching a clock, watching the second hand ticking away. Starting at number twelve, as it ticks away, I begin to realize that every second of hypnosis to me will represent many minutes of peaceful rest and relaxation where my mind and body become rejuvenated, regenerated, knowing that there is harmony between mind, body, and personality now. And this harmony will carry over into my daily life. I will be able to express myself more easily and naturally, being able to say what I feel like saying and do what I feel like doing.

In a few moments, I am going to begin awakening myself, using my awakening process, counting from zero to five. With each number, I will become more and more awake. Physically, I will be relaxed. Emotionally, I will feel calm, peaceful, and happy. Mentally, I will feel very sharp, very alert, thinking very clearly.

And now I begin to awaken myself. Zero, one, two, slowly and gently coming up. Three, feeling more relaxed as I awaken. Four, and four becomes a very alert number. I begin to feel my breathing changing. The movement of my eyes taking place. And now, five. Wide awake. Wide awake. Wide. Wide. Wide awake.

Countering sexual difficulties with self-hypnosis

6

Self-hypnosis is an extension of your natural suggestibility. As you saw in Chapter 4, problems of the past, often long buried in your subconscious, can emerge as difficulties during your most intimate moments. You know that you desire sexual relations. You know that sex is the most natural source of pleasure that can be shared by two people. Yet you have had problems because of early childhood teachings, an unpleasant experience with the opposite sex, or some similar difficulty.

For years, you have let your natural suggestibility work against you to a degree. You let a subconscious reminder of the past cause premature or retarded ejaculation, if you are a man, or difficulty with climax or orgasm, if you are a woman, among numerous other problems. With self-hypnosis, we are going to change this by letting your suggestibility reinforce the positive in your life, not the negative.

Some of you may have tried to use will power in the past. You approached a member of the opposite sex with the idea that if you wanted a relationship enough, you could have it. Yet despite this determination, something always went wrong, even if it was only your developing a fear to risk the emotional pain which could result should the relationship go sour.

Will power simply does not work with serious problems. Will power is only effective with minor considerations where pleasure is the eventual result.

Theoretically, sex always leads to pleasure and thus will power should be an important factor. However, your subconscious mind is frequently recalling a past event which caused you pain or emotional discomfort. Subconsciously you fear that the end result of the relationship you are seeking will be the same rejection, humiliation, guilt, or other difficulty from the past. Your conscious determination is not adequate to overcome the subtle pressures of the subconscious. Thus your will power does not work.

The self-hypnosis you learned in the previous chapter will enable you to reach your subconscious and influence it towards your positive goals. We have found in our studies that subconscious thoughts are seven to nine times more powerful than the conscious awareness. Thus when you change the subconscious thought process, you are tapping seven to nine times more power over your life than conscious determination will allow.

You have probably seen self-hypnosis used by others for purposes other than influencing their sex lives. For example, have you ever watched a weight lifter during international competition? Notice how, before lifting an unusually heavy weight, he or she will close the eyes and seem to meditate for a moment. If you look closely, there is even some rapid eye movement such as occurs when you are in the hypnotic state. What these individuals are doing is meditating briefly, effectively tapping into their subconscious minds, before lifting the weight. They are using self-hypnosis to overcome the conscious resistance to that weight. Thus, the conscious mind may be saying,

> I am determined to lift this weight. It is extremely heavy. It weighs more than I do. I didn't get much sleep last night. I've never lifted this much before. Everyone's watching me. I don't know if I can do it, but I'm determined to do it. And what if I make a fool of myself and can't budge it because it's an awfully heavy weight?

The subconscious mind, when tapped through the meditating or self-hypnosis process, is being told

> I can lift this weight. I have been lifting weights almost this heavy ten times or more. All I have to do is lift this weight once. I know that when I do ten repetitions of one weight, I can just as easily lift a much heavier weight once. This weight will be no problem. I will lift it and win this contest easily. It will be a simple, smooth movement and the audience will be applauding my success. Here I go!

And the weight is lifted flawlessly. The reason is that all the "rational" negatives which crept into the positive thinking approach were eliminated by the seven to nine times more powerful subconscious motivation.

Self-hypnosis is actually nothing more than allowing the mind to narrow its focus to one concern. All other thoughts are eliminated. Then you can tap that inner essence which allows you to change your subconscious thinking and overcome obstacles in your life. It is used by people who practice meditation, fractional relaxation, and numerous other techniques which go by a variety of names. It is a controlled thought process and, with it, you will be able to overcome all the concerns you are facing regarding your sexual performance.

The conscious awareness of self-hypnosis as a tool for change means that you are developing a regimented approach to tapping your subconscious. Most forms of meditation are not consistent. Self-hypnosis follows a strict pattern which you learned in the previous chapter. It is simple, easy for anyone to use and, most importantly, becomes faster with practice. You probably took several minutes to practice self-hypnosis each time you tried it while studying Chapter 5. Yet the more you practice, the faster you can enter the self-hypnotic state. You will find that when you begin adapting it to your sex life, you will be able to put yourself under in a few seconds, your partner never realizing the change which has come over you.

The other difference between self-hypnosis and forms of meditation or relaxation is that you have a mechanism or procedure for stopping the self-hypnosis. You have a set form for putting yourself into this state and a set pattern for bringing yourself out. This gives you constant control of the experience and prevents any negative experiences from affecting your action.

There will be times when you will want to stay in the hypnotic state through orgasm or climax. There will be other times when you use the self-hypnosis to prepare you for sex, then come out of the state during intercourse. Each problem is slightly different, as you will see shortly. Just remember that even in self-hypnosis, you have conscious awareness and control. You will have full sexual feelings with your partner and will not be like a zombie during the sex act. You will have as much pleasure and give as much pleasure to your partner as if you were not in self-hypnosis, but you will be able to control circumstances which, in the past, prevented full sexual enjoyment. Then, when you have changed your subconscious mind so that you no longer need the extra suggestion possible only by being in the self-hypnotic state, you will stop using self-hypnosis during the sex act. You will have changed so completely that your conscious mind can act to bring you pleasure without the extra support.

You also do not have to have a current sex partner to utilize self-hypnosis for change. You can begin using the self-hypnosis to provide a subconscious suggestion which will be put into effect when you do have a relationship. For example, a man with premature ejaculation may suggest to himself that he will be able to delay his orgasm for two minutes longer than he has been able to do in the past. He will follow the format you will learn shortly, suggesting that when he does have intercourse, there will be a two-minute delay compared with his past experience. He will also want to use self-hypnosis just before the actual act, but then the self-hypnosis will be serving to reinforce the previous suggestions. It will become directed towards a specific woman rather than a general condition.

Premature Ejaculation

As we discussed in Chapter 4, one of the most common problems for men is premature ejaculation. The man ejaculates almost at the instant of penetration. This means that there is such enhanced stimulation that just the extra contact of intercourse results in an orgasm. If you have this problem, you are going to use the self-hypnosis you have learned to delay your release.

Basically, you are going to suggest to yourself that, upon penetrating, you will feel a numbness in the head of the penis. You will give yourself this suggestion before you have sex. This can be just a few minutes before the sex act, such as while you are in the bathroom, or at some period before you will be going to bed with a woman. Some men, knowing they will be having sex the next day, give themselves the suggestion the night before. Other men may do it an hour before. One of my patients tried it when he picked up a woman at a bar, giving himself the suggestion as they entered her apartment.

Married men and couples who are living together have the easiest time. They can plan the sex act so that the man will know when they are going to have intercourse. Then he can begin making the suggestions he will need to decrease the stimulation and delay orgasm.

The numbness will not affect the erection or the pleasure you can give your sex partner. It will simply reduce the stimulation so that there is a delay in your ejaculation until you consciously make a change by giving a key word. Your suggestion creates the delay; then the saying of the word, and this can be any word you wish, will allow the full sensation and ejaculation.

For example, you might go into self-hypnosis, then make the following suggestion:

> I am going to feel a numbness in the head of my penis when I penetrate. The numbness will stay there until I say the word to myself 'ejaculate.' When I say the word, the numbness will disappear and the stimulation will become extreme and I will feel myself preparing to ejaculate.

You will practice this self-hypnotic suggestion several times. Some men like to do this twice a day, as well as shortly before they are going to have intercourse. They may do it once in the morning, upon arising from sleep, and once in the evening. The more you practice this, the more deeply you will change your subconscious mind. After several repetitions, the ability to control your release will become automatic, your subconscious mind having been changed.

You know from the earlier chapter that you are either a physical sexual or an emotional sexual. The way in which you suggest changes to yourself will vary with your sexual personality. The physical male needs a slightly different form of suggestion than the emotional male to avoid increasing stimulation instead of decreasing it.

The physical sexual male will enter self-hypnosis, think of the partner, and say,

> The next time I have sex with Mary (or whomever), the moment I enter, I will feel a numbness in the head of my penis. Even though I will feel the stimulation in other areas of my penis, the head of my penis will remain fairly numb until I say the word 'ejaculate.' When I say the word 'ejaculate,' the numbness will lift and I will ejaculate.

During this time, the physical sexual male will not use any visualization techniques. He will simply make this suggestion to himself.

If you are an emotional sexual male, you will make the same statements to yourelf while under self-hypnosis. However, you will also visualize the sex act. You will picture yourself with your sex partner, becoming aroused, then penetrating and not ejaculating until you say your key word. All of this will be lived through the fantasy of the mental image.

The reason for the difference between the two is that the physical sexual male may actually increase his stimulation through the visualization. He may become overly stimulated, thus increasing the chance for premature ejaculation instead of alleviating the problem through the suggestions. The emotional sexual male needs the visualization technique in order to truly enhance his subconscious suggestion. However, he will not have his stimulation increased in this manner.

An alternative to the suggestion of penis numbness is to specify a length of time. Some men find it easiest to be more precise about their ejaculation. They suggest that they will have this numbness for two minutes after they penetrate. Then the numbness will lift; they will feel the enhanced stimulation and say their key word. This will be repeated until the two minute time is automatic.

Next the man will add more time. The new suggestion will be for a numbness lasting three minutes before lifting. Then he may go to four or five minutes, gradually increasing the time after the success of the previous suggestion is routine. This is especially helpful for the man who has had a serious problem with premature ejaculation and comes so quickly that a gradual slowing seems to work best.

There should be no concern about satisfying your sex partner during this time. Some men want to suggest to themselves that they will not release until the woman has climaxed or has an orgasm. This requires too great an awareness of the orgasm instead of the enjoyment of the sex act. It also requires the man to be aware of when the woman has climaxed, something which may not be realistic. He might ask her, but there is the chance that either she would not tell him the truth or that the truth would be upsetting.

Instead, concentrate on learning to prolong intercourse before ejaculation, increasing the time slowly. After you have done this, you will be able to stay long enough to provide mutual sexual pleasure. And, as you learned earlier, when you are mutually stimulating each other, the message units become overloaded and orgasm or climax occurs automatically. Admittedly, this means that your sex partner may not be satisfied at first. You may be delaying your ejaculation, but not delaying it quite long enough. However, since you are working to increase that delay, this problem, if it exists at all, will continue for only a few days. Then you will be cured for life and never again have this type of concern.

Note: The changes you will achieve through self-hypnosis are permanent ones. You are altering your subconscious. However, you are also fighting years of negative thoughts. It is a wise idea to regularly use self-hypnosis to reinforce the new suggestion. The more often you use reinforcement for any of the problems corrected in this chapter, the stronger your subconscious. Thus I always tell my patients that once the change seems permanent, it helps if approximately every ten times they have sex, they use the self-hypnosis technique once. This one-time-in-ten reinforcement constantly enhances the subconscious. Then, after a few weeks, you can eliminate the use of the self-hypnosis for this problem since the problem will no longer exist. You will use it again only if you become worried that it might be returning.

The Nonorgasmic Woman

Some women are unable to achieve orgasm or climax when they have sex. This is one of the most common problems reported to therapists and one which is easily corrected through self-hypnotic suggestions.

The nonorgasmic woman, and remember that we are talking about women who are unable to climax or orgasm, needs to enhance her fantasy stage of the sex act. She needs to be able to overload her mind with message units about sex so that there is a physical reaction. If you have this problem, you will be handling the cure in stages, starting with increasing your mental stimulation, then increasing your physical awareness once aroused. As I have stressed before, if you can enjoy the stimulation of sex, that enjoyment eventually leads to an overload of message units which results in an orgasm or climax. When you concentrate only on the orgasm or climax, you become so tense that you do not enjoy the physical stimulation. This prevents that message overload and greatly delays or prevents your having orgasm. Thus this exercise is meant to help you enjoy the act, a situation which always leads to either climax or orgasm.

I want you to start by using fantasy while under hypnosis. You are going to do something which may seem a little odd at first, depending on how you were raised. You are going to fantasize about whatever and whomever seems arousing to you. Never mind that this may not be your sex partner. Never mind that the act involved may be one which you would never do. The important point is that you are are using this to begin learning the overload of the fantasy stage of sex. You are going to use your mind to create a circumstance which increases your physical desire.

You may be the type of woman who was raised to think that fantasy was wrong. Or you may have been taught that certain types of fantasies were wrong for nice girls to have. You also may have been taught that sex other than under certain circumstances, such as for procreation, was improper. If this is the case, then it will help you to desensitize yourself before starting the fantasy stage of correcting your problem.

Enter self-hypnosis and, while in this state, tell yourself positive statements concerning sex. You might say something such as,

> Sex is a natural act between two adults. Sex is pleasurable. I am going to enjoy being aroused by (name the man or, if you have no ongoing partner, say something such as "a man I find special"). Sex can be enjoyed at any time we are together. Sex is natural. Sex is fun. Sex is right for me.

Whatever you choose to say, you are simply desensitizing yourself from the past.

Again, since you are trying to enhance your sex drive, both physical and emotional sexual women should use visualization. You can start by imagining the man in bed with you if you are comfortable with this. However, if you need desensitization, usually you will want to start fully clothed. You may just be looking at the man from afar, enjoying his appearance. Then he will be closer and closer. Next you will be touching, perhaps kissing each other. Take one step at a time until you can fantasize yourself being naked and desiring his body.

Once the desensitization is complete, assuming that you need it, you should concentrate on the change for your subconscious which will begin leading you to the achievement of orgasm or climax. Start with the fantasy stage and involve anyone you want.

Many of my women patients enjoy fantasizing about someone other than their spouse or lover. This may be a movie star, a politician, an athlete, or even a casual acquaintance whom they find exciting. Often it is an actor as he appeared in a particular movie role. The fantasy does not mean that they actually want a different man. They are using the fantasy to enhance stimulation and this is perfectly healthy. You are not going to act out your fantasy and you possibly would not want to do it. However, fantasy adds to sexual stimulation and this is your immediate concern.

Harriet told me that she used a fantasy of the actor Burt Reynolds.

> I fantasized that he saw me in the supermarket and followed me home. He knew I was married, but that didn't matter. He had to have me, even at the cost of his career. In my fantasy, he waits until my husband goes to work, then he knocks on the door, declaring undying love for me when I answer.
>
> I am shocked. I invite him inside because I don't know what the neighbors will think if they see Burt Reynolds at my door. I tell him I'm married and faithful to my husband. Then he smothers my protests with kisses, carrying me into the bedroom. I try to resist, but his kissing has left me too weak. He gently removes our clothing and I am no longer able to resist. We are on the bed together and I am aroused in spite of myself. He enters me and I have the greatest experience I have ever had.

Ann has a different fantasy. She imagines two men fighting over her, eventually both trying to have her. Sometimes she settles for just one of them. Other times her fantasy involves the two of them in bed with her, each trying to outdo the other in keeping her aroused.

Linda is at a rodeo with her boyfriend when a cowboy lassoes her, taking her on his horse to a ranch before anyone can find them. He gently ties her to the bed, then begins touching her body until she cannot stand anymore. When he frees her, they passionately embrace and he enters her.

Some women have very simple fantasies with subtle touching, such as a man meeting them in a restaurant, buying them wine, and making chaste but obvious moves to tell them they are exciting. Others may have an affair with a boss or an employee. If there is gentle rape, the most common fantasy, some women imagine themselves as the aggressor and others are the helpless, but always desiring, victim. They may stay with one sex partner or have a chain of lovers at an orgy.

There are three stages needed to begin changing the non-orgasmic (nonclimax) condition for a woman. The first is to go into self-hypnosis and let the fantasy run loose. It does not matter what your fantasy might be, as you have seen. Any sexual fantasy which works is a good one. Should there be any concern about your past emotional reactions to it all, then you will want to desensitize yourself as shown. The important point is that you continue the fantasy.

Next you will want to begin feeling your physical reaction to the fantasy you are creating. Again, go into self-hypnosis, this time having the fantasy but also trying to think of your body. Experience the fantasy, then let your mind drift to your body. Are you becoming warmer? Is your heart rate changing? Are you lubricating at all or feeling any urges? Think about your body's reaction and try to experience as much as you can from the physical side of the fantasy. Then return to your fantasy, again thinking about the sex in any way you choose. Finally, take yourself out of self-hypnosis as shown so that you are again going about your normal activities.

Repeat this approach several times until you can consistently feel a physical change. The method will always be the same: Enter self-hypnosis, experience the fantasy, let the fantasy transfer to an awareness of your physical reaction, return to the fantasy, and then make yourself become wide awake.

Once you have this consistency, you should increase the physical sensation in a controlled circumstance. The easiest way to accomplish this is through the use of a bathtub filled with warm water. The warmth of the water will envelop you, raising your body temperature, giving you pleasant physical sensations, and affecting your genitals.

Enter the bathtub when you have a quiet time alone. As you soak in the pleasant, warm water, put yourself into self-hypnosis again. Enjoy whatever fantasy adds to your erotic thoughts, then become aware of your physical body. Experience the movement of the water around your genital areas. The water and its movement will enhance the physical sensations generated by the fantasy. Then continue the fantasy while feeling the water. The touch of the water coupled with the fantasy will cause more message units to enter your brain. You will have the intense fantasy and the uncontrolled stimulation building an ever more pleasant experience until you naturally orgasm or climax.

Remember that you must not worry about reaching an orgasm or climax. It will come eventually. That is not something over which you have control. All you want to do is increase the mental and physical stimulation and self-awareness through the combination of fantasy and the sensation of the water. The more you do this, the more aroused you become naturally. At some point, and it may be your first time, your fifth, or almost any other, you will find that there is a pleasant, natural climax. It comes without your control as a result of the overload of sensation.

This third stage can also be enjoyed with your sex partner. Both of you can enter the bathtub or he can be on the outside of the tub, gently touching you while you are fantasizing. The stimulation of the partner adds to the stimulation of the warmth of the water, further increasing the message units to the brain.

Now begin to have sex with your partner after first entering a state of self-hypnosis. Use your fantasy of whatever person or groups of people you desire. You want to have as many message units related to sex reaching your brain as possible. The fantasy will build the feelings as your partner is touching you during foreplay.

While still in the foreplay stage, open your eyes and become aware of your sex partner. Enjoy what he is doing and, if you desire, also place him in your fantasy. Some women simply enjoy exactly what is going on. Others are constantly aware of the partner but their fantasies include actions which he may not be making at the moment. They might fantasize that he is going to penetrate after forcing them into the bedroom for gentle rape. Or they might fantasize that he was one of several men who fought for her favors and he was the victor who is now claiming his prize. There are probably as many different ways to fantasize as there are women. What matters is that this time the fantasy is directed towards the sex partner.

Try to enjoy all the physical experiences you are having. You have the fantasy to help trigger the physical awareness. You have the reality of your ongoing partner. And you have the physical sensations of his touch on your body enhanced by the fantasy. Either during this experience or after two or three attempts to experience sex in this manner, you will find yourself naturally reaching climax or orgasm. This will happen automatically and not with conscious control. You simply enjoy the total pleasures of the fantasy and the touching, concentrating on the experience, not any particular goal. Enjoy the man, the loving, the total sensations of what you are doing, and you will find that the orgasm or climax are reached simultaneously.

Repeat this exercise three or four times so that you are comfortably and consistently reaching climax or orgasm. Then try to have sex without entering a state of self-hypnosis. Relax and enjoy it, taking the time to experience the touch of your partner. You can still fantasize about him if you desire when preparing to have sex. Fantasy is always an important advance stage and quite separate from what you have done with the self-hypnosis. The only difference is that you will be using fantasy without the self-hypnosis.

Usually you will continue to have orgasm or climax. There may be slight nervousness the first time which you overcome with one or two repetitions of the sex act without self-hypnosis. Should there be any problem, this is a minor concern. Return to the use of self-hypnosis for the pleasurable experience and practice that way a few more times. Then again try without the self-hypnosis. In almost every case, I have found that should there be a need for a second time, that second use of the self-hypnosis leads to adequate reinforcement so that it is not needed again. However, if you find that a third attempt is necessary or that you want to periodically reinforce the change in your subconscious through the use of self-hypnosis every ten or more times you make love, this is fine.

There is one problem which can arise for the woman who is unable to have an orgasm or climax. This occurs when the inability to have such pleasure comes from anger or guilt. For example, a woman who enjoyed sex with a man who suddenly left her for someone else may harbor great anger towards men in general. Not only is she upset by the shabby way in which she was treated, but she is also afraid of being hurt that way again. She will not want to risk becoming happily sexually involved with another man, even if she is lubricating or seems ready for sex, because she is afraid of being hurt again. Failure to have an orgasm, even though she has lubricated and he has penetrated comfortably for both, is a subconscious conrol.

Obviously, the current sex partner is not the previous one who acted so improperly. It is also obvious that the woman feeling this anger truly wants a relationship, yet is afraid of a repeat of the previous one. She knows intellectually that the situation is different but there is a subconscious control to change before she can effectively utilize the approach to orgasm you have just learned.

The simplest way to handle this problem is to enter a state of self-hypnosis and visualize the current sex partner. Then, depending upon your past, say whatever positive statements will help you. For example, during this visualization process, you may say,

> I want to have sex with this man. This man is exciting to me. Having sex with this man is a good experience. This man will bring me pleasure. I will enjoy having sex with this man. Having sex with him is a proper thing for me to do. It is right and enjoyable and I am going to have fun with him. I feel sex is perfectly natural.

Other statements which are helpful include:

> Sex is a natural experience. All men and women enjoy sex. It is a pleasurable act. It is a natural act. I am going to enjoy sex like all others because it is a good experience, a proper experience, a natural expression of pleasure between a man and woman.

It is usually best for only the emotional sexual to visualize the sex partner. The physical sexual female need only say these logical statements. She does not have to add the visualization because she will accept the positive ideas without this extra step. The emotional sexual needs the extra stimulation of the visualization in order for it to work. However, both types of sexual personalities can use the visualization if desired because it does help to increase the desire phase.

You are giving yourself all positive suggestions. You are not trying to analyze your anger or your guilt. You are simply recognizing that the situation you are in with this man is a new one and you are not letting the past act to hold you in its control. There are times when there may be more serious relationship problems, such as extreme anger towards the current sex partner. This usually manifests itself in your having the inability to lubricate, a somewhat different matter than not being able to reach an orgasm or climax. Because of this, the desensitization techniques for this problem are discussed later in this chapter in relation to nonlubrication.

Retarded Ejaculation

Retarded ejaculation is a problem that often results from a sense of guilt or some other emotional problem. The man is obviously stimulated or he would not have been able to have an erection. Penetration is no problem, yet after penetration, something happens mentally which causes him to desensitize himself to the stimulation of the female. In order to counter this problem, it is important to enhance the physical sensations and to eliminate the emotional problem preventing full enjoyment of the sex act.

If you are a physical sexual male, you are going to want to be able to counter what is actually an emotional problem. The suppressed emotions, usually including guilt, must be corrected. This requires tapping into that portion of the brain that handles the emotions since the brain is actually divided by functions. The right half of the brain handles emotions. The left half of the brain handles logical reasoning. If you fall in love with someone and are greatly aroused by her presence, desiring to spend your life with her just because she is so beautiful and exciting, you have used your right brain. Your reaction is strictly emotional and based on instinct and sensations rather than logic. However, if you then sit down and, before acting on these feelings, start weighing her qualities as a person—her intelligence, mutual interests, possible career conflicts, long-term goals, and the like—before committing yourself, you have used your left brain.

When you take a physical action while in hypnosis, it can affect the ease with which you are able to tap into your emotions. The simplest physical action is the tightening of the hand opposite the side of the brain you wish to reach. Clenching your left fist while under self-hypnosis makes it easier for you to experience change in the right side of your brain, the emotions-handling side. Clench your right fist and you will more easily activate the logical reasoning of the left side of the brain. I know this sounds slightly confusing, but it does work.

Retarded ejaculation is usually caused by some unconscious emotional guilt. This can range from religious and family teachings about sex (it is wrong to have sex for anything but procreation is one message often conveyed in childhood and carried subconsciously into adulthood) to an upsetting emotional experience during sex. By entering self-hypnosis and clenching the left fist, anything you are working to change which has an emotional cause will be more easily handled.

The physical sexual male should enter self-hypnosis with his left fist clenched to help push the suggestions into the right side of the brain. Then say to yourself,

> I am going to become very stimulated by the idea of penetration of the female. (Use a name if desired.) Having sex is an exciting idea to me. I am letting go all misconceptions about this behavior. I don't need any type of restrictions like guilt any longer. I am going to begin to enhance and feel the stimulation with women. I am going to be able to ejaculate, feel extensive physical pleasure, and enjoy the sexual act.

The emotional sexual male should enter hypnosis in the exact same manner, using the same suggestions. However, the emotional sexual male should also visualize a sex partner. He should see himself having a pleasurable sex act, penetrating and reaching an ejaculation fairly quickly.

After using this exercise in self-hypnosis several times, you will go to a second stage of preparation. Once again enter the self-hypnotic state, your left hand clenched to help enhance the activation of the right side of the brain (the emotions). Now suggest to yourself that the next time you start to penetrate a woman, you will immediately feel a high degree of excitation in the penis area. Again, the emotional sexual male should also fantasize the female while attempting this exercise.

Because retarded ejaculation requires much greater stimulation than in the past, it is important to heighten sexual excitement in much the same way as a woman needs to do this when she has been unable to reach orgasm or climax. This means that you will also want to enter a state of self-hypnosis before your intercourse and stay in that state through ejaculation.

Once you have entered this state of self-hypnosis, begin fantasizing any act which you find exciting. This might be gentle rape of your partner or of yourself. Some men like to fantasize having two women seducing them. Others like the fantasy of looking out a window and seeing a sex act being performed. Still others enjoy the idea of two women fondling each other before touching the man. Again, there are no limits to what you might fantasize and no fantasy that is wrong. You can enjoy the fantasy with your sex partner as the woman or imagine any woman—an actress, singer, neighbor, co-worker, or anyone else—as the person with whom you are having sex. The important point is to increase your excitement. Later, once you have become comfortable with the faster ejaculation, you will switch to a fantasy which only involves your sex partner.

It will help to have a post-hypnotic suggestion implanted in your subconscious. Once you are ready to have sex without being in a state of self-hypnosis, you are going to practice a reinforcement technique through the post-hypnotic concept. During times other than when you are having sex, enter self-hypnosis. Then suggest to yourself that when you enter the female, you will begin to feel the sensation forming. As soon as you feel this sensation, use the key word "ejaculate." When you say the word, you will feel the sensation increasing to an overwhelming experience, at which time you will ejaculate.

Repeat this process several times. You will not be going into self-hypnosis during the sex act. You will be using a suggestion for a post-hypnotic experience. This will further reinforce the subconscious.

Now that you are gaining control over your orgasm, it is also important to desensitize yourself from the past. It is quite likely that you are aware of what has caused you the emotional distress which has revealed itself through the retarded ejaculation. This memory has not only been painful, it has been difficult for you to overcome. You know that the past is over, yet you are still being victimized by it.

To counter this problem, enter a state of self-hypnosis and think about the personal relationship which led to the retarded ejaculation. The emotional sexual should visualize the circumstances which occurred, the physical sexual need only be aware of the problem. Then say to yourself, "I am going to release from my thoughts any restrictions I have felt about (name the problem and/or person). I am going to free from my thoughts any embarrassment I might have about the sex act."

Many men who experience retarded ejaculation have fears that they are latent homosexuals. This is *not* the case, but they are remembering a past experience to which they gave too great an importance. This may have been an urge they had while in high school or it may even be a single act involving another male for which they feel unnecessarily guilty. Instead of recognizing that this was a normal experience which many men may have, they become convinced that they were bad and are inherently unable to truly maintain a relationship with a woman.

To counter these fears, enter self-hypnosis and visualize a woman you desire. Then say to yourself, "I enjoy sex with a female. Sex with a female is extremely pleasurable. I do not enjoy the idea of sex with a man. It is not my behavior. I enjoy women." Again, if you are a physical sexual, you do not need to add the visualization.

The Problem of Rejection

One reason a man may have retarded ejaculation is because he was put down by a woman in the past. Rejection is a major cause of problems, though the strength of the reaction to rejection is greatest for the physical sexual man or woman. Both sexes, and both sexual personalities, may have to cope with rejection and the way to do this will differ with your sexual personality.

The emotional sexual man or woman is likely to have handled rejection with pain but not with a lingering, destructive anger. The emotional sexual need only place himself or herself into self-hypnosis and visualize a new sex partner. Then make all the positive statements towards this person necessary to increase sexual desire. "I am going to enjoy sex with (name). Sex with (name) is a pleasurable act. I am going to release myself from the past so I can truly delight in (name). I am greatly aroused by (name) and will enjoy our relationship." The person who was a problem in the past is simply ignored. You move forward without bothering about what came before.

This is not the case with the physical sexual man or woman. If you are a physical sexual, you are going to have to do more to desensitize yourself.

Again place yourself into a state of self-hypnosis. If you are a physical male who has been rejected, your problem might range from retarded ejaculations to an inability to have an erection. While in self-hypnosis, have both your hands palms upward on your lap. Think about the woman who rejected you and begin tightening your left hand. Now suggest to yourself that you are going to transfer all those emotions about the woman to your left brain where you can deal logically with the problem of the past. Now tighten your right hand and release the left hand. This will transfer the thoughts to the left brain where you can deal with them logically.

Now, with the thought of the woman in the past safely in your left side of the brain, say, "The relationship with (name) is over. I cannot allow myself to let that relationship continue to give me pain." Next switch to thoughts of another woman. Make the positive statements towards her mentioned for the emotional sexual.

This process also works for the emotional sexual who experienced such a strong rejection that he needs desensitization before he can think positively about a new woman. The only difference is that he should visualize first the woman who caused him pain and then the woman about whom he wants to think positively.

Women who have been rejected should follow this same procedure with the man. Again, you are removing the man from the emotional side of the brain to the physical or logical side of the brain. Again, follow the procedures for emotional and physical sexuals. This is a technique which works equally well for men and women.

Difficulty with Lubrication

There are many women who experience difficulty with lubrication. This is different from the woman who is unable to achieve orgasm or climax, since such women may be able to orgasm when artificially lubricated. However, the majority of women who are unable to lubricate are also unlikely to achieve orgasm or climax when artificially lubricated.

As you have learned, the lubrication of a woman is the natural result of the fantasy stage of sex. Without this mental excitation, lubrication cannot be created. The sex act is experienced as a way of pacifying her partner, but it is not something she is enjoying. The pain is eliminated by the artificial lubrication, but the pleasure is prevented because there is no mental stimulation.

The difficulty with lubrication does not have to happen during your first sexual experiences. I have often found that a woman can enjoy sex for years with no difficulty in lubricating. Then a conflict will arise which affects her subconscious and suddenly she stops lubricating. In one instance, this occurred after seven years of marriage, a period of time during which sex was regularly enjoyed.

The reason why failure to lubricate can occur after conflict is because the fantasy stage is not properly utilized. The woman focuses on all the negative feelings and/or the negative experience which led to the conflict. She is not concentrating on the fantasy and advanced stimulation which precedes intercourse and allows an overload of the brain to carry into the physical experience of lubrication.

For example, imagine yourself naked with your sex partner. You discovered that he had an affair with someone at his office many months before. He is extremely upset that it occurred, you know that he loves you, and you also know that there is no way he will ever consider doing something like that again so long as you are married to him. He has begged for forgiveness and done everything in his power to prove he is contrite.

You forgave your partner, and you may have had sex with him a number of times since that discovery. Yet you are still extremely angry and you have not fully dealt with that fact. Your mental process, as he begins to stroke you, might go something like the following:

He's stroking my back. That always felt good to me. He knows just where to touch and how much pressure to use to get me to melt. Any moment I'm really going to get turned on. He's so good at manipulating me.

Manipulating me. Like the way he kept me satisfied when he was running around, screwing her. I wonder if he touched her the same way. I wonder if he knows all her little secret spots.

I hate the idea that his hands were touching her like this. I wonder what she was like in bed. I wonder if she could get him going like me. That little...

And so it goes. The woman is letting her anger override the mental process that would otherwise begin increasing her arousal. She does want the man, but this held-over anger is destroying the relationship.

At other times, there is leftover guilt. The woman experienced an affair or did something else that she felt was wrong and became uncomfortable with herself. The failure to lubricate is a way of punishing herself.

Sometimes the anger is less obvious, as in the case of Linda, a patient of mine who had been dating a married man for five years. She was a physical sexual who was overwhelmed by the man. She adored him and believed that he would one day leave his wife. The marriage was shaky, they seemed to be leading separate lives, and he gave every indication of truly loving Linda.

The man was serious about Linda, but extremely weak. He was unable to make a clean break with his wife, whom he did not love, and a commitment to Linda. He kept promising that he would, yet it did not happen.

For five years, Linda was the other woman. Linda felt herself almost a convenience at times and constantly wondered if she was doing the right thing by staying with the man. Then everything changed. He developed his courage, made a clean break with his wife, obtained a divorce, and moved in with Linda.

The man thought everything should be blissful. He had finally proven his affection and his intentions. It had taken him a long time to build his courage, but when he acted, he did exactly what he had been promising. He was a delighted man.

After a couple of days of their living together, Linda could not lubricate. She had enjoyed an extremely active sex life with him for five years, yet when they could finally have everything which they had been planning, she could no longer be comfortable with him. That was when she came to see me.

Linda was angry. She realized that, although she loved the man, he was so weak that she had been victimized for the previous five years. She had always been available. She had restructured her life to fit his circumstances. And when he had finally gotten the courage to do what he claimed he wanted to do for so long, he expected everything to be perfect.

The anger took hold of Linda's subconscious. She wanted to punish him in some way for what he had done to her, though she loved him enough that she did not want to lose him. The best way she could accomplish her goals was to deny him one of the pleasures they shared—sex. Her ceasing to lubricate was an unconscious way of punishing him for what he had done to her. She did not realize the cause and effect, though she did realize her anger.

Such a situation required two approaches. The first was talking with the man. Linda needed to explain her feelings and let him understand how she perceived what they had experienced together in the past. There was no way he could undo what had occurred, but he needed to know that such indecision in their relationship together could never be repeated.

Talking with her lover was not enough. Even though Linda expressed her anger and worked through her feelings on a conscious level, there were still subconscious pressures at work. To handle this process, she went into self-hypnosis and visualized herself being angry with her lover.

The visual fantasy was far more violent than she would ever do normally. She yelled at him, she ranted and raved, she picked him up bodily and heaved him out the window. For five years she felt she had degraded herself waiting for him to make up his mind and then, when he finally got a divorce, he came to her expecting nothing but the gravy of the relationship. She did want him and there was nothing more to be said in person than had already been discussed, but there was plenty she could do under self-hypnosis.

After working through several rather violent fantasies, Linda told herself that she would vent her anger through dreams. Each night, when she went to sleep, all the anger that remained would be vented through the dream process. Then, when she was finished working through all this, she brought herself out of self-hypnosis.

Linda had to repeat these actions several different times. In between, she would force herself to be with her lover, although they did not have sex. They talked about her anger, though she did not share her extreme fantasy violence. They healed their relationship, the venting dreams and the self-hypnosis acting to alter her subconscious. By the third time she made the suggestion to vent her anger through her dreams, Linda found herself lubricating again. The problem was resolved.

Had Linda been a different type of individual, she might have chosen to leave the man with whom she was so angry. However, she truly loved him and simply wanted to express her anger and frustration now that her wait was finally over. Had she not talked with him, the venting through self-hypnosis would have worked as well, though it would have taken longer. There also could have been other problems with the relationship since the man was having difficulties as well. He was weak, insecure, and left the familiar situation of wife and home in order to be with the woman he had come to love. When she stopped lubricating, the rejection terrified him. He was afraid he had made a mistake, even though he had not been in love with his wife for several years.

Under such circumstances, the male can also have a sexual problem. This may range from impotence to retarded ejaculation. The solutions for him will be the same as those mentioned in this chapter for the identical problems, even though the cause is somewhat unusual.

A second major cause for failure to lubricate is the inability to fantasize. If this is your problem, then you will not be able to create mental images which lead to having sex. This seems an insurmountable problem when you first experience it. After all, if you cannot fantasize, then how can you get through the fantasy stage of the sex act?

The reality is that everyone can learn to fantasize because everyone does fantasize. Women who are unable to do so are actually reacting to some trauma in their past. A situation occurred at some point that they found so upsetting that they choose not to remember. They have either been punishing themselves or fleeing from a memory and thus do not allow themselves the opportunity to start the procedure leading to lubrication and enjoyable sex.

The easiest way to learn what may have happened if you are unable to fantasize is to rely upon what is known as an ideomotor response. Under hypnosis, you can ask yourself questions and receive an answer through the triggering of a physical response. There are many ways to do this, though the simplest one is to suggest to yourself that you will answer "yes" or "no" by the raising of the appropriate finger. For example, you place your hands on your lap or on the arms of a chair. If the question is to be answered with "yes," you will raise your left index finger. If the question is to be answered "no," you will raise your right index finger.

To understand how this works, let us take the example of Melinda, a clerk in city government. She was an emotional sexual who had never lubricated. She also had never had an orgasm or a climax. When I encouraged her to fantasize, she told me that she had never been able to do it. She said she didn't even know how to begin.

I continued to encourage Melinda to fantasize, but my encouragement made her irritable. She didn't like the idea of trying to do it. She felt uncomfortable and became angry when I pressed. There was obviously something she was repressing, though I didn't know what it might be.

I had Melinda enter into a state of self-hypnosis such as you have learned to do. Then I had her suggest to herself that when she asked herself questions, the answers would be revealed through the raising of the appropriate index finger. This ideomotor response would accurately reflect her thought process.

Melinda first said to herself, "Do I know why I don't lubricate?" She raised her left index finger to indicate a "yes" answer.

"Am I willing to expose the feeling which has prevented me from lubricating?" Her right index finger was raised. No, she was not willing to expose it.

"Do I want to be happy?" The left index finger, again. She wanted to be happy.

"Would I like to be able to lubricate and function sexually?" The left index finger. Yes, she would.

"Since I want all this to happen, do I know why I don't want to expose the reason I am not lubricating?" "Yes" was the reply.

"Am I willing to tell the reason?" "Yes," again.

"Will I be willing to tell the reason in response to a direct question concerning what is bothering me?" The answer was "no" this time.

"Am I willing to vent it out through my dreams?" The answer was "yes."

There are two ways to vent through dreams. The first is to suggest that you will remember the problem. You do not have to remember an early problem to vent its influence from your mind. Often I find that this awareness helps. The situation is over and you are not going to cause yourself leftover pain and guilt for something that cannot be undone. It is time to move forward, the venting giving you that release. The memory may satisfy your curiosity and give you a better self-understanding, but it is not critical.

Tonight I am going to go home, I am going to go to bed at my usual time, and I am going to have an extremely restful sleep. During that sleep, I am going to vent out what happened in my dream. The dream will show me why I cannot fantasize.

Melinda did dream that night. When she awakened, she remembered the time when she was a young girl and had been with her older cousin. The two of them had had sex together for several months. She had enjoyed this sex immensely.

At the end of a year together, the sex stopped. They both developed an understanding that somehow it was wrong. Yet Melinda had enjoyed the sex. She had been having a wonderful time and this fact filled her with guilt.

The full memory returned. Her parents had become suspicious of what was going on. They took her to their church and made her confess what she had done. She was humiliated by the experience and overwhelmed with guilt. It was not that she had had sex with this cousin that seemed so terrible, but rather the fact that she enjoyed it. Immediately she was turned off to sex.

Melinda was shocked by her discovery. She had not remembered the incident. It had been so long since it happened that she had put it completely from her mind. Yet it was obvious that this was the reason why she had experienced the difficulty with sex. It was the residual guilt that had prevented her from lubricating or fantasizing.

The next step was for Melinda to return to self-hypnosis, during which she said to herself, "I have exposed the cause of why I wasn't lubricating. I am now an adult and not a little girl. I have vented it out through my dreams. I now can start lubricating." She repeated this two or three times and then started lubricating immediately, even before she had come out of the self-hypnotic state.

Once Melinda lubricated, it was obvious that she would have no trouble enjoying sex. Yet there was still the question of fantasy. She had to learn the mental preparation for sex which she had suppressed for so long.

Melinda placed herself back under self-hypnosis. She fantasized herself in the midst of a group of friendly people. She was enjoying herself with the people. It did not matter who they were. There was nothing sexual about the experience. She was just enjoying herself with pleasant company.

This fantasy was an easy one to use because it offered nothing threatening to Melinda. She could relax and enjoy it.

Next we tried some other fantasies. The ones Melinda used may or may not be ones with which you are comfortable. If these are different from ones you would enjoy, you can select anything which becomes more intimate.

Melinda, for example, fantasized seeing a couple making love. She started with them kissing and touching, then worked her fantasy until she was watching them have pleasant intercourse. She also fantasized that she was seeing a sex film, all the action on the screen reflecting sex acts she was comfortable viewing others do.

You might find that you are not comfortable with the viewing of another's sex act. You might want to fantasize just the hints of intimacy and tenderness between them. You should let your fantasy go only so far as you enjoy, gradually increasing as you are comfortable with that increase.

The reason for fantasizing about someone else is because that image does not seem personally threatening. You are not putting yourself into a fantasy position of having sex. You are a watcher, an innocent voyeur who is enjoying an erotic image.

Next Melinda fantasized that she was involved with some man who was stimulating to her. The partner could be anyone. It might be someone she knew and found attractive. It might be a man she was dating. It might be a movie star or some hero from fiction. The important point was that now she was personally involved. She was with the man and the man was interested in her.

Soon Melinda was fantasizing about sex with a man. She indulged any whim she might have had, always being the woman who was enjoying intercourse at the end of the fantasy. She also was fantasizing about the involvement of the man she loved, a man with whom she had never lubricated in the past because of the problems she had experienced, then suppressed, when young.

The change in Melinda was intense. She told me that the moment she arrived at her lover's apartment she began to lubricate. She was aroused at the prospect of sex with him, even before she was inside and they were together. Sex presented no further problems for her.

Many times a woman will know the cause for her difficulty lubricating. The cause is remembered, unlike Melinda's case where she had pushed it from her mind. But because the cause is uncomfortable, it is not discussed and continues to have a bad effect on her. This occurs after any unpleasant experience, from rape to humiliation as a teenager when caught masturbating.

There was the case of Ann, a happily married woman who had been enjoying sex with her husband for seven years. Then, without any obvious warning, the lubrication stopped. She came to see me for therapy and I suggested that she use the ideomotor reflex to find the cause of the problem.

"Do I know the reason I stopped lubricating?" Ann asked herself when under self-hypnosis. Her index finger indicated "yes"; she did know.

"Am I willing to expose this reason to myself?" The answer was "yes" again.

"Do I know how I will expose this?" This time her other index finger indicated "no."

"Can I suggest that I will remember it?" At that instant there was no need for the index finger to indicate a response. That simple question brought the memory instantly to mind.

The memory was a simple one, yet it shows how we can carry guilt for actions which might seem trivial under other circumstances. Ann had been at an office party where everyone was drinking fairly heavily. She was close to her boss and had always been attracted to him. In the relaxed atmosphere, in the midst of friendly co-workers, all away from their spouses, she became aroused by her boss's friendliness. They touched and, in a light moment, the boss kissed her, causing her to become sexually aroused.

Ann felt tremendously guilty. She had always believed it was wrong to be sexually involved with any man other than her husband. Just the idea that she was aroused and could sense herself lubricating filled her with shame. The moment she experienced the lubrication, she forced her thoughts to change, cutting off the lubrication. Unfortunately she carried this guilt home and punished herself by continuing to be unable to lubricate.

There was obviously no reason for Ann to feel guilty. She did nothing terrible. The situation was a natural one under the circumstances and she had exercised control to keep it from getting out of hand.

Ann again entered self-hypnosis, this time armed with her new understanding of herself. She told herself:

> I have exposed the reason I have been unable to lubricate. It was not an abnormal act. I was under the influence of alcohol and in an unusual circumstance. What happened was human nature, and I maintained control. I did not cheat on my husband. I have no reason to feel guilty about what I experienced.

Now suppose you have this problem, but your situation is somewhat different from Ann's. Suppose you had this experience and went ahead and had sex with the man. In your mind you have reason to feel guilty because you commited an act you feel is wrong.

The reality is that after something like this happens, you cannot undo it. The action may be wrong for you, but it is over. You must accept this fact and move forward, a situation you can most effectively handle through self-hypnosis. This time you will say:

> Hanging onto this guilt can do me absolutely no good. Exposing what I have done to my husband will not do me any good. It will not help our relationship. It will not make amends for what I did. I must recognize now that it happened, it was a mistake, but it's history. I don't need to suffer with it any longer. I have paid enough for the act and the guilt I felt. I want to let it go.

You may have to repeat this self-hypnotism a few times. However, once you have absolved yourself in this way, you can move forward and again lubricate. You stop being a victim of your past.

There are rare circumstances where the mind does not want to deal with what happened. You want to fantasize. You want to lubricate. You want to enjoy a sexual relationship with a man. Yet the ideomotor response remains negative, your mind trying to suppress the memory and thus keep you a prisoner of your past.

Should this happen, and it is a rare circumstance, you will need to take charge of your mind under self-hypnosis. This time you will tell yourself,

> I am going to fantasize. I am going to lubricate. I am going to vent out the cause of my problem through a dream. I do not have to remember what happened, but I will vent out its control through a dream. Then I will be able to fantasize. I will be able to lubricate. I will be able to have an enjoyable sex life.

Later you can also go into self-hypnosis and tell yourself to fantasize. "I will fantasize about men. I will fantasize about sex."

The fantasies you will then want to suggest to yourself will usually involve gentle rape. Both men and women relate to this fantasy because it handles most of the mental needs of foreplay. If you are embarrassed by sex or fighting past suggestions by parents that nice girls don't enjoy sex, you can become the willing but helpless victim of the man you desire. In your fantasy, he is always tender, loving, gentle, but over-powering. He might simply overwhelm you with his amorous advances, leaving you so weak with his caress that he is able to remove your clothing without your being able to struggle. He might carry you to bed, physically overpowering you, though again without any pain. Or he might go so far as to tie you to the bed, the bindings loose enough to be comfortable yet secure enough so that your struggles are useless.

This same fantasy of being overpowered and helpless is one used by some men as well. It is a natural one which satisfies both your desires and your previous teachings. You are enjoying sex, but you are not initiating sex. You have not violated the parental argument against doing it because the sex act is happening to you. You are helpless to stop it so you can enjoy the experience without guilt.

The opposite fantasy is that you are controlling the situation. You are the person who is initiating the gentle rape. You are taking the man or woman of your fantasy. You are creating the helpless emotions which lead to intercourse. You are tying the person to the bed so that nothing happens except that you have a firm control of the situation. However you are making it occur in your fantasy; you are the one in full control of the experience.

One of the two rape fantasies is comfortable for the majority of men and women. One of them will allow a fantasy sexual experience without guilt. One of them will help you reach the point where you can enjoy the fantasy stage and easily lubricate.

The rape fantasy is also safe because a fantasy of simply enjoying sex may be something you want but are ashamed to want. Everyone has desires, though some people feel that the desire may be wrong. Having someone else do it to you allows you to enjoy it without guilt.

Another approach is the voyeur fantasy. You are not involved with the sex act, but you are watching someone else engage in it. Again, this is not personal. There is no guilt because you are not the one having the pleasure. Yet the idea gives you pleasure and the viewing of the act helps you to begin lubricating.

Naturally, where there is this guilt of participation, it is best to follow up the fantasy with a desensitization suggestion. This is where you tell yourself the positive aspects of sex, explaining that you are an adult, you are not a victim of the past, that sex is enjoyable and a natural act between adults. This self-hypnosis technique will also help move you forward in your relationship.

There are some individuals who stop lubricating out of boredom. Something happens in the relationship which causes the sex drive to diminish. Perhaps the woman desires a different man, one whom she cannot have. The man she is with is seen as someone comfortable, a friend who no longer seems an exciting lover. Yet since the other man is not available, he is all there is.

At other times, there may be pressures from work which make the woman tired, gradually overwhelming her and diminishing the sex drive. Or the sex life may have become such a routine that it is no longer interesting or arousing. Or the partner might have some habit which has been tolerated but has been growing increasingly unpleasant in her mind. Whatever the circumstances, the drive is seemingly gone.

The reality of this circumstance is that one of two things is happening. Either the relationship has actually died, the couple in need of separating, or it is simply time for a change in the relationship. The woman truly does want to stay with the man but needs a way to rejuvenate the sex life. This is a time to use the ideomotor reflex to help understand what is happening.

Under self-hypnosis, use the ideomotor suggestion, saying, "Do I care about (name)?" "Do I want to continue with my relationship with (name)?" So long as the answers are "yes," then you know that you need to change the relationship to increase the fantasy stage and encourage arousal. If the answer is "no," then you must face the fact that it may be time for a separation, divorce, or intense counseling, depending upon which you think is best for you.

Should you find that there is boredom, it is time to begin reviving the fantasy stage through self-hypnosis. The boredom naturally serves to reduce the libido. This sex drive can be returned by using self-hypnosis to experience more of the fantasy stage. You increase your desire and reactivate the relationship.

Naturally you may want to also talk with your lover if there are unpleasant habits involved. Yet even when this is the case, you will want to work on the fantasy stage while restoring the sex drive. You can also engage in variations of the sex act which are enjoyable for you both. Just remember that no matter what changes you make and no matter what sex games you choose to play, the first stage involves increasing the fantasy.

The Problem of Male Impotence

Some men are impotent with women but, when they have taken the test to determine whether or not they experienced nocturnal erections, always break the tissue paper. This means that such an individual does not have a medical problem. He is being victimized by an experience in his past.

The reasons why you may have this problem are varied. Often it is not the result of some major circumstance, some big, dramatic trauma. Rather, it can be a series of little events, all of which have come to affect you.

As a general rule, the use of self-hypnosis is fastest when you work towards correcting the symptom of a problem. This brings the fastest results when possible. Should attacking the symptom not be productive, then you must go for the cause. Thus this is also the way you will approach your problem with impotence.

The first step for the man who is experiencing impotence is to work to enhance the sexual excitement. Remember, if this is your problem, you are capable of having an erection. You have proven that at night, probably having the erection during an erotic dream which you did not remember upon awakening. Thus, if you can increase your sexual fantasies under self-hypnosis, you may correct your problem.

Go into self-hypnosis and begin fantasizing in the hypnotic state. This fantasy will involve two different stages. You will start by having a fantasy about the partner with whom you are going to have sex. This can be any fantasy you desire. It might involve nothing more than looking at her naked body, perhaps kissing and caressing her. Or it might be an elaborate fantasy involving anything from gentle rape to being a voyeur while she and another woman touch each other, then work to stimulate you.

Shift from this fantasy where the partner is the one you will be having to a fantasy involving anyone else. This might be a movie star, a co-worker you find attractive, or anyone else. This is someone you find sexually exciting, though you have no way of pursuing the relationship. The person might simply be an actress whose role you enjoy or someone who is happily married whom you do not know well but who you find intriguing. You can fantasize anything you want. There might be an orgy with several naked women, all of whom are desperate for your body. You might be gently raped by two women or you might be the one who is carrying off this person. There might be a romantic scene you are recreating, perhaps with soft music, wine, a Swiss chalet, a giant, canopied, circular bed, gypsy violins, a gentle snowfall, and all the other features of a Hollywood romantic spectacular. Or there might be a rugged adventure in the Old West. It does not matter what you do so long as it is exciting to you.

Remember that you may have a sense of guilt for such a sexual adventure. This is because of early training which you recognize intellectually is unrealistic. However, it carries over and you feel that you are somehow being naughty, bad, or even dirty for thinking about such things.

There are two realities which you need to face. The first is the fact that there is nothing wrong with any sex act between two consenting adults as long as neither party is physically hurt. Everyone has fantasies which they may try to act out or they may suppress. Normal individuals do not want to rape someone when raping means causing pain and forcing someone to submit to discomfort against their will. However, normal individuals do enjoy gentle rape where one of the partners is overpowered with great delight. A man or woman may tie a sex partner to the bed, making certain he or she is quite comfortable, yet helpless enough that all he or she can do is sense the touch of the other. Or a person may seek to be taken in this way or some variation, such as simply being held down or weakened through kissing before being forced back on the bed. There is no whipping, beating, or any other violence. If there actually is a tying down, it is done in a way that will not hurt the other person and the sex partner who is rendered helpless is never left alone to insure safety. It is a sex game which might be acted out in reality or fantasy. And the same is true with all other sex games.

Knowing that this is normal, natural, and enjoyable when mutually desired, there is nothing wrong with such fantasies. Also, there is the undeniable fact that sex is fun and a method for a man and woman to enjoy each other completely, quite apart from procreation. Yet, there are warnings some of us have received in the past, either from well-meaning parents with limited knowledge or from religious groups with rather extreme views. These warnings can lead us to have difficulty with sex as adults.

Also, there can be other hurts affecting your ability to get an erection. Humiliation by a woman or some other problem which is either long forgotten or suppressed rather than eliminated may do this.

Should this be the case with you, you can use the same desensitization techniques discussed for women earlier in this chapter. Place yourself in self-hypnosis and make positive suggestions concerning sex, visualizing your sex partner or any woman you desire, as you make suggestions to yourself. The emotional sexual may also wish to visualize the actual sex act at the same time, though this is not essential with the physical sexual. Then say something to the effect of:

> I enjoy sex with women (or name a specific person). Sex is extremely pleasurable. Sex is a good thing to enjoy. I am not going to be bothered by past ideas. I am not going to be a victim of old suggestions from my parents and others. I am going to have great pleasure with women (or name). I am going to become sexually aroused by (name). I am going to have an erection and enjoy entering my sex partner. It is a good experience. It is the most natural sharing a man and woman can have.

Then, after you have desensitized the ideas form the past, continue with the fantasies we have been discussing. Switch back and forth between the woman who is your sex partner and the woman who is your fantasy partner. This might be several women and any sex act is possible. The important point for you, if you have had problems with impotence, is that under self-hypnosis, you continue to alternate between the two to greatly enhance your fantasy. This should continue until you sense the start of an erection.

Once you begin to feel this start, which is usually the engorgement of blood that precedes the full stiffening process, you will make a new suggestion to yourself. "I am going to develop an erection. I am going to develop this erection while I am fantasizing in this hypnotic state."

This effort should begin to increase your sex drive. Continue it until you are able to have an erection while under self-hypnosis.

Remember that until you feel even the slight change in your penis from the early engorgement of blood, you should be using whatever fantasies are exciting for you. Then, once you have this sensation, suggest that you will have an erection while still in the self-hypnotic state, before continuing with the alternating fantasies.

Once you have had your erection, you will use self-hypnosis when enjoying sex with your partner. Practice your fantasies before your evening with her. You will be having erections the same way you have learned, each time building your confidence and awareness that you are no longer impotent. Then, just before you have sex, place yourself in a self-hypnotic state and return to your fantasy of the other woman or women.

I know that you may feel a little guilty about this, though you need not be overly concerned. You are learning to have sex so that you may have a normal, fulfilling relationship. Do not be concerned when it is necessary to fantasize about others. This is similar to the problem of the woman who cannot have an orgasm, and the method for correction is the same. You will want to tap into the ideomotor reflex, letting your subconscious mind handle the problem.

Once again place yourself under self-hypnosis. Tell yourself that you are going to ask yourself questions and you will signal the answers with your fingers. Again, you can have your left index finger raise for a "yes" and the right for a "no." Then say to yourself, "Do I know the reason why I cannot develop an erection?" The answer will usually be "yes."

"Is my mind ready to release and expose this thing to me?" Again, the answer will usually be positive.

"Will it come to my memory now?" If the mind says "yes," then you will have the memory. If the mind says "no," then you will say, "Then I will expose it through my dreams. Is that acceptable?"

Should the mind say "yes," then you will say, "I will sleep very deeply, very soundly tonight and I will vent out the original cause of why I cannot get an erection in my early morning dreams. I will remember the dreams and the reason why I cannot get an erection."

If the mind says "no," you simply implant more powerful suggestions.

I will remember to vent out the cause through my dreams. I will sleep very deeply, very soundly tonight and I will vent out the original cause of why I cannot get an erection. It is time for me to move forward with my life. I will do this by venting out in my dream and I will remember when I awaken in the morning.

Once you have the memory, and it will come back to you, go back into self-hypnosis and say to yourself, "I have vented out the cause of my failure to have an erection. I am now free from this condition. Now, as I fantasize my partner, I am going to develop an erection." By repeating this suggestion, you will have an erection.

Should your mind tell you that you will not remember, it may be that you choose not to remember the specific situation. In this case, you will demand that you be free from the past. You tell yourself that you will have an erection, you will not be controlled by past experience. Then you say,

> I will vent the problem through my dreams. I will vent out the cause of my failure to have an erection. I do not have to remember these dreams, but I will vent out the cause. I will be able to have an erection when I am with my partner.

Once you are aware of the problem from the past, you will want to desensitize yourself to the experience. It does not matter what it may have been. Sometimes the problem was caused by an incestuous act you experienced. You may have had someone make a homosexual approach to you. Or you might be widowed and, every time you start to have relations with a new woman, you have guilt which shows itself by remembering your late wife.

The reality of all such experiences is that they are over. You are not living in the past and the situation is not what it was. If you were a victim of someone else, this does not mean that there is anything wrong with you. If you tried a sex act of which you are now ashamed, it does not mean that you are bad or that you are homosexual, incestuous, and so on. And if you are a widower who keeps seeing your ex-wife, this does not matter because she is dead. You are alive and it is important for you to move forward. You can have more than one healthy relationship in your life. So long as you are alive, you need other people and this includes sex with another woman about whom you care.

Place yourself in hypnosis and visualize the person and/or the act which has led you to have an inability to have an erection. Then say, "I am going to desensitize myself from the deviated act." Or, "I am going to desensitize myself from the influence of my late wife when it comes to sex." Or, "I am going to desensitize myself ... (name the circumstance)." You specifically name the situation and inform your subconscious that you are going to desensitize yourself. Review the scene and repeat the suggestion.

In the case of the ex-wife, you might add,

> I am going to stop denying her death. She is gone. There is no reason for me to continue living in the past. I am going to accept her death. I am going to mark a closure on our time together since she is dead and I need to get my life back.

The same situation exists with each circumstance. You do not need to analyze why you did whatever it was that made you have so much trouble. You do not have to concern yourself with the reasons why you were susceptible to a homosexual act while a teenager, abuse from someone, or anything else. You simply accept the fact that it happened, that it is over, and that you are moving forward with your life. You make these positive suggestions under self-hypnosis and move forward.

There are some circumstances where a man maintains an erection, then loses it at the moment of penetration. This is not an orgasm but just the loss of the erection. This is almost always the result of guilt, is identical to the problem of having no erection, and should be treated in the same manner.

General Performance Anxiety

The problem of general performance anxiety affects both men and women. It comes from being uncertain about your sexual skills, your ability to please the other person, your ability to be as creative or sophisticated or knowledgeable as you think the other person desires.

For example, suppose you are a woman who is a virgin and are involved with a man who is sexually experienced. Your assumption is that other women have taught him all manner of ways to enjoy sex. You are convinced that there are special methods for touching him, certain acts which will arouse him, and other secrets which come from repeated sexual experience. You may be completely naive or you may have read a book or two, such as *The Joy of Sex,* to learn technique. But book learning is not the same as practical application of technique. You are scared that you will not be able to excite him and, if you can excite him, that you will not be able to give him as much satisfaction as he is accustomed to enjoying.

The same problem exists for the male, though his concerns are more obvious. The woman will lubricate so the penetration by her partner will be enjoyable. The man, on the other hand, fears not gaining an erection at all. He is frightened that he will not be stiff enough or remain hard while his sex partner has fun. His concerns are even greater.

I had performance anxiety after having had sex for ten years," explained Margo, whose unhappy marriage ended almost a year before she had sex with another man. "My ex-husband and I had developed almost a ritual. The days of the week when we would have sex, the way in which he would enter me, and every move we made had become rote. It wasn't pleasant. It wasn't unpleasant. It simply happened and served as a physical release. It had been much better when we were first married, but at the end it was a habit. The only pleasant experience we shared.

Then I met Wayne and everything was different. He was gentle, loving, and sophisticated. When we reached a relationship where sex seemed the natural extension, I was scared to death. I didn't want things to be as they were with my ex-husband, and I had not experienced sex any other way in so long that I was afraid I wouldn't give him pleasure. I wanted to be clever, creative, to drive him up a wall with desire, yet I didn't think I was any good. I didn't know what to do. I was sexually experienced and felt like it was my first time. I was certain I would fail him.

A woman actually has little problem from the general anxiety condition. She will lubricate and penetration is no problem for the man. Also, in the early stages of a relationship, both parties are nervous enough that she need not worry about preventing him from enjoying sex. Then, after the second or third sexual experience, the relationship has deepened enough that the anxiety disappears.

This is an important point to remember. General performance anxiety is an experience which ends quickly for both parties. It comes during the first stages of the sexual experience, then is cured by familiarity with that person. After going to bed together just two or three times, the anxiety leaves. You realize that you are finding mutual enjoyment and there is more of an openness concerning personal desires and any variety in the sex act that you might desire.

If you are a woman experiencing this problem, you do not need to worry about the cure since time is the effective cure. You will be lubricating, you will not be experiencing pain, and the man need never know that there was ever any concern. You can use self-hypnosis to suggest to yourself that you will be comfortable during the sex act, you will enjoy it, and other positive statements. Remember that you do not have a serious problem and it will correct itself with two or three sexual experiences no matter what you might do. The man will not be aware of the circumstance and you need not be overly concerned.

If you are a man, you may need to use self-hypnosis to avoid being embarrassed by this condition. You routinely have an erection but may not have one under the stress of the new relationship during the first time or two you have sex. As with the woman, time takes care of the difficulty. However, knowing this fact does not stop your showing what will be an obvious problem by your lack of erection. Thus, you will need to use self-hypnosis.

There are other manifestations of this situation. You might have premature ejaculation, reaching a climax the moment you enter your sex partner. Some men climax during the foreplay or have a delayed orgasm. The fact that you might be experienced with a large number of women prior to this relationship means nothing. It is the special nature of the new relationship, the closeness you feel, that raises the level of anxiety. Time corrects this problem, but this is of little consequence.

To counter this problem, place yourself into a state of self-hypnosis and visualize yourself having sex with the woman about whom you have performance anxiety. Visualize yourself performing without problems. Now suggest to yourself that you are excited, you are enjoying the sex act. All these positive statements will help you through this anxiety.

You can keep yourself in the state of self-hypnosis during the sex act the first time or two. This will help you be more comfortable and aroused. You can suggest to yourself how aroused you are while in the early stages of the sex act so that you have no problem with erection.

At the same time, you will be desensitizing yourself to past problems if necessary. For example, if you have been unpleasantly divorced, or if you are widowed and feeling guilty, you can suggest that moving forward is necessary. You use the suggestion that the past is over and you will not be affected by it any more. You must go forward with your life and your relationships. Having sex with this new woman is a good experience, a proper experience, an experience you can let yourself enjoy.

This approach is also important when you are being affected by a past circumstance which only hurts performance with a special woman. I once had a professional athlete, an extremely famous individual known for his rugged good looks, who was experiencing performance problems with the one woman about whom he had become serious. He had had casual sex with a number of women in the past. He had never had trouble performing, but he also had not taken the experiences seriously. They were moments of sexual pleasure with friendly fans— not women with whom he might consider making his life.

It turned out, when the athlete used self-hypnosis to understand his problem, that as a high school athlete he had gone to bed with a girl who was extremely attractive and also very free with her favors. All the boys on the team had been to bed with her. However, when this man had had his turn, she had rejected him. She called him a "bum lay" and ridiculed his manhood. She then spread the word that he wasn't any good at sex.

Time passed and the athlete thought he had overcome the past. He enjoyed casual sex without problems. However, what he did not realize was that he subconsciously harbored a fear that when he became serious about a woman, she would also think he was a "bum lay." It was this subconscious fear that surfaced to haunt him and create his performance anxiety. He thus used the desensitizing approach you have learned to rid himself of the past and the self-hypnosis technique described to perform successfully during the early days of his intimate relationship. The result was successful sex, which has helped him to realize a long-term relationship he has been enjoying with the special woman in his life.

Had this situation occurred more frequently with women, he would have had to desensitize himself each time. It would have been necessary for him to use self-hypnosis and mentally think back to each woman with whom he had had a problem. Then he would review the relationship and desensitize himself to that past experience. He would do this over and over again, touching upon each one until he could function normally in his current and future experiences.

Women Who Climax and Wish to Orgasm

I cannot stress enough that not all women orgasm. The idea of the orgasm for a woman is one of the tragic myths of stories about sex. A woman who has an enjoyable sexual experience and is physically and emotionally healthy may either have an orgasm or climax. The climax is a highly pleasurable cessation of the sex act. It is not the rolling sensation of the orgasm which involves both the clitoris and the vagina, yet it is one natural way to end the sex act.

Popular literature, misinformed men, and even women themselves will place undue pressure on the idea that the orgasm is the only proper end to the sex act. So long as you at least climax, you are having sexual pleasure.

Having stressed the fact that climax is normal, it is also necessary to remember that an orgasm is so much fun that women who climax may want to try to experience this additional response. This is quite possible and you can do it with the use of self-hypnosis. You will be using the natural law of association to transfer climax into orgasm.

Generally the emotional sexual woman and the extreme (eighty percent or higher) physical sexual woman are likely to want to have greater sensation than the climax. During the sex act, they are narrowing their focus onto the clitoris where they are feeling stimulation. When the climax occurs, the previous stimulation and/or their expectations concerning the way they would feel with a climax is so intense that they are disappointed by the result. Such women want to increase their experience through the development of an orgasm.

The first step in changing your sexual experience is to stop feeling guilty or frustrated by the fact that you are achieving climax. Enter self-hypnosis and suggest to yourself that a climax is a very normal, acceptable ending for the sex act. It is an enjoyable experience. It is a natural experience. It is an experience that results from your sexual personality.

Repeat this approach at least a half dozen times in order to remove the anxiety you have been feeling. You want to convince your mind that your experience is normal and that you do not have to change to be a complete woman. Any change you make will be by choice, not by a sense of guilt. This also eliminates the overconscious control of the release which has been keeping the mind and body focused on the climax.

Next, you will begin self-hypnosis during which you fantasize that you are with a man who excites you. You fantasize that he is stimulating your manually and/or orally, getting you more and more aroused. Then you fantasize that you release at the moment the man penetrates you.

Repeat this fantasy several times, always under self-hypnosis. This should be done when you are alone, always having your fantasy release at the moment of penetration.

Next put yourself into a state of self-hypnosis when you are with your sex partner. Fantasize about the sensations of manual stimulation. Think about the oral and/or manual stimulation from your fantasy, all the time that your sex partner is also stimulating you. Your fantasy might be about him or it might be about some other individual you find exciting. What you are trying to do is increase the message units to your brain by having the dual stimulation of the fantasy and the actual physical touching.

This overload of message units to the brain causes a natural transference from the clitoris to the vaginal area. You are effectively extending the physical area of your feelings, leading to the vaginal involvement which is necessary for orgasm.

The overload is necessary in order to experience a vaginal release. This release may not occur the first time or second time you try this approach. You may have to use self-hypnosis in this manner several times with your partner. However, eventually you will experience the vaginal release, not just the climax with the clitoris.

Once you experience the vaginal release, the next time you have sex, you will not place yourself in self-hypnosis. You will have sex while fantasizing in much the same way you did under hypnosis. This will increase the message units and may lead to the vaginal involvement again. If it does not, then you will place yourself under self-hypnosis for your next sexual experience, repeating the fantasy as before. Repeat this until you have a vaginal release again.

Eventually you will find that you naturally have a vaginal release. This may take a dozen or more times, but this is all right. Remember that you have a natural tendency to climax and you are expanding your physical awareness in order to involve the vagina. This will take some effort, though it will be quite pleasurable and will eventually enable you to achieve the result you desire.

Each time you have sex in this way, you are increasing your receptiveness to the message units of sex. This will lead to the overload that increases the strength of the release. You will have gained the option to experience both types of possible releases for the sex act. You may even want to return to having just a climax, and thus you will stop fantasizing and using self-hypnosis towards this end.

Reducing the Intensity of Your Orgasm

Some women do not have the problem of wanting to increase their release by going from climax to orgasm. These women have extremely intense orgasms and usually multiple orgasms. However, instead of gaining pleasure from their intensity, they find themselves upset by the sensations they are experiencing.

For example, some women have extremely rapid release upon penetration by the male. They do not delay the orgasm long enough or sustain the orgasm so that the male can share some of their sensation. The orgasm instantly follows the foreplay and they would like to delay it until the man has some pleasure following his penetration.

There is also a condition among some women which results in the release of a heavy substance when they are stimulated vaginally and clitorally by the hand. This release occurs during foreplay and is perfectly natural for them, but is a heavier release than many other women have and thus can be a turn-off for some men. This is a physically obvious release which is almost as if the woman urinated, though she did not. It is an intense, slightly thin lubricant.

Some therapists have thought that this overlubrication was actually a female ejaculation, the equivalent to a male's. There were even efforts made to find out how all women could experience the sensation. However, the reality is that this is simply an intense lubrication in response to stimulation, an extreme version of the natural lubrication process prior to penetration. It is most likely to occur with emotional sexual females who have not experienced a release in the past. The first few times they release, it is almost as though there is a build-up from the past which causes such extreme lubrication.

This release of liquid is almost as intense as a man's release of liquid. It is not urine but is a substance which comes from the accumulation of the natural lubrication women release. Thus it is necessary to minimize the stimulation because such women are receiving too much stimulation too soon.

If you are experiencing this problem, enter self-hypnosis. Now you will give yourself a suggestion that you will feel a minimal amount of stimulation until you start thinking "orgasm." You must think this or verbalize it in your mind, the stimulation becoming very strong at that time. It is at this moment that the release occurs.

The idea is to prolong the reduced stimulation you are creating. Instead of enhancing your excitement, you are delaying it. This will take practice, but eventually you will be able to minimize the lubrication compared with what you have been experiencing. Then, when you give yourself the key word to orgasm, you will immediately release. This reduces the lubrication and eliminates or minimizes the problem you have been experiencing.

This is a difficult condition to break. If you have this problem, you are probably bothered by it and want to end it quickly. Most men whose partners experience this circumstance do not mind it. However, the women want to stop it quickly and this may not happen. You will need time, but the self-hypnosis will work with a little practice.

For those who have not encountered this difficulty, it is extremely upsetting for the women who have. Sometimes the release can be so intense that it is painful. At other times, it is extremely upsetting. For example, one woman who came to see me was thirty-two years old and had had, by her own estimate perhaps twenty different sexual relationships with men. In every case, she had orgasmed before penetration. The moment the man touched the vaginal area, she would release, her body being soaked. This proved so strong and personally embarrassing that she decided to give up sex.

I had her enter hypnosis and begin minimizing the feelings by going through the stages of arousal and release in her mind. She suggested to herself that she would lose the intense arousal at each stage of the relationship. In her fantasy, she would first think of the early arousal, stopping herself before she could become too excited. Then she would fantasize the penetration stage, again preventing the release. This prolonged her feelings while the man became comfortable. Finally, she fantasized releasing just as he did.

This is not to say that she was trying for a simultaneous orgasm with the man. This is one of those fantasy goals which means nothing and causes hardship. It is always best for the woman to experience a release before the man. This is because the man may not be able to regain his erection and, without the erection, he cannot satisfy the woman. It is only in a case such as that of my patient where simultaneous release is realistic and desirable since it is totally within her control after she practices for a while.

The Clinical Orgasm

It is possible to create what is known as a clinical orgasm, an experience which is desired by women who have the opposite problem from the woman in our example. This is a method for overloading the brain with sexual messages until there is a climax or orgasm.

To do this, a woman enters a state of self-hypnosis. You will not be touching yourself, but you will visualize and fantasize the sexual act. You begin to suggest to yourself that you are feeling sexual. You suggest that your body temperature is becoming warmer. You feel that your breathing is starting to increase. You begin to feel little contractions in your vaginal area. You feel yourself lubricating. You feel some shakiness down your legs and into your feet. You begin to feel that your body is developing a momentum of the breathing becoming deeper and deeper. Your body is responding and becoming warmer and warmer and warmer as you visualize and fantasize the sexual act you are in. You can use any fantasy you desire. You continue until there is an automatic release. This enhances feelings more than masturbation and can serve as a substitute for masturbation for those women who feel guilty or dirty touching their bodies.

This procedure can be done by any woman who wants to enhance her sexual release. This becomes very comfortable and automatic.

For Men and Women

Now that you understand the counters to sexual problems, you will be able to use self-hypnosis for any difficulty which might have prevented you from having full sexual enjoyment. Should you have a problem which is somewhat different from the ones described, you can follow the procedures you have learned, adapting the suggestions you make for your own needs. This will result in a more complete, more fulfilling sex life now and always.

How to make
a good sex life better

7

No matter how good your sex life has become now that you have an understanding of your sexual personality and the ways in which you can use self-hypnosis to correct the problems of the past, everyone would sometimes like to have it even better. You have learned how to use fantasy to increase your arousal. You have seen how, if you are a woman, you can go from climax to orgasm or reduce the intensity of your orgasm if that is your concern. However, there are some other methods you can use to increase your pleasure with your sexual partner.

Using Your Sexual Personality

If you are a physical sexual man or woman, it is quite likely that your partner will be your natural opposite, an emotional sexual. This means that he or she will be slower to arouse. Your body changes make you ready for intercourse almost from the start of foreplay. Your partner, on the other hand, will take longer.

It is always best for the physical sexual to begin arousing the emotional sexual during the early stages of foreplay. Unlike yourself, the emotional sexual is not aroused by direct genital and erogenous zone contact prior to the final stages of foreplay. Instead, stroke away from the erogenous zones. Touch the back, the neck, the legs, always stroking away from the penis or vagina. Only after there is strong arousal should you make contact with the genital area.

Your partner will not be as comfortable with talk during sex as you will be. You are likely to get aroused by talking sexually during intercourse, quite possibly using slang terms for sex. Your partner, on the other hand, may be most comfortable being silent during intercourse.

When you talk with your partner, you might express your feelings in more general terms. Talk of love and/or the pleasure you are feeling. Avoid slang terms for sex during intercourse itself because this may be a turn-off.

If you are a female, it is best for you to be satisfied first, and this is true for the emotional female as well. Bringing the woman to climax or orgasm before the man assures that both partners will be satisfied.

Your natural tendency as a physical sexual man or woman is to want to prolong the sex act. You may have felt at one time or another that you wanted to enjoy sex all night. Your desires are often for a more involved foreplay and intercourse than your partner. He or she can learn to extend the pleasure, and you can help by starting the foreplay with the emotional sexual before having yourself aroused. However, at the end of the sex act, your partner may wish to arise from the bed instead of clinging.

One answer, and this is easier for the physical female with an emotional male lover, is to plan your sex so that you sleep or rest in each other's arms after release. The male body chemistry is such that it is fairly easy for him to drift off to sleep after sex. However, it is only the emotional male who fully releases during orgasm. The physical male will retain some of the semen so that he can repeat the sex act within a few minutes. There is also the problem of the emotional female likely to want to arise from bed after climax or orgasm so this works best with the emotional male/physical female combination.

The emotional sexual will need to work on developing mental as well as physical foreplay. Encourage your physical sexual partner to begin foreplay by stimulating you, then switch to your arousing your partner prior to intercourse. Again, the male should bring the female to climax or orgasm before he releases.

Your partner is turned on by sex talk when he or she is a physical sexual. Try to use slang words for sex during foreplay and, if you are comfortable with them, during intercourse. Usually, your expressing yourself with terms which might be slightly uncomfortable for you will be a turn-on to the physical sexual. Talking about sex and the pleasure you are getting, especially using slang expressions, heightens your partner's enjoyment.

Recognize that you have a cycle for sex. Some people, usually physical sexuals, are on at least a one-day cycle. This means they enjoy sex daily. Others, and usually these are emotional sexuals, may want sex strongly only every two or three days.

The emotional female/physical male can adjust to each other because the emotional female can learn to have sex daily even though her strongest cravings may be every other day or every third day. The physical female with an emotional male partner will have a more difficult time, but she can also help him increase his frequency slightly by taking the sexual initiative when he is not on a cycle day. Just remember that both emotional sexual men and women will also be comfortable with less sex than the physical counterpart and it will be the physical who may have to make the greater adjustment. This is a minor problem, but recognizing it in advance will avoid any possible frustration.

Same Sexuality Partners

If you do not have an ongoing sex partner at the moment, you might find that the same sexuality partner or one slightly less strong (a seventy percent physical with a sixty percent physical, for example, instead of a seventy percent physical with a seventy percent emotional) can be rewarding. This is because you will be on the same cycle days and follow identical patterns. There are fewer adjustments to make.

When there are May/December romances, the ones that are successful combine similar sex drives. An older woman who is a physical sexual marrying a younger male physical sexual can work extremely well. She will welcome his activity and, as he ages, he will still have a stronger sex drive than the same age emotional sexual male.

The reverse is also true. An older emotional sexual male can have an extremely enjoyable relationship with a younger emotional sexual woman. Again, they can learn to cycle their sex to a common pattern, being able to please each other easily throughout life. This is not likely to happen with an older emotional sexual male and a younger physical sexual female.

Admittedly, the chemistry of a couple is always strongest when they are opposites. Yet, if you are seeking a relationship, consider the same sexual personality for maximum compatibility with minimum interpersonal adjustment.

There is a difference in the sexual desires of an emotional sexual and physical sexual. The physical sexual wants the greatest frequency of sex and is always ready to go to bed with his or her lover. Yet once in bed, the sex act is fairly straightforward with little variety.

The emotional sexual male or female may have less of a sex drive but more varied interests. It is the emotional who will be more likely to want to try different positions, oral sex, and perhaps sexy clothing. The physical sexual can heighten the emotional's sex drive by trying such variations to please the partner. At the same time, the emotional sexual can improve the relationship by not forcing the pursuit of great sexual variety when the partner is not comfortable with such an act.

Open communication about sex is also essential. The self-hypnosis you have learned will enable you to heighten your awareness and increase your enjoyment. Talking with your partner, sharing your desires, your feelings, and your pleasures, as well as listening to your partner's needs and desires, will help solidify your relationship. The greater the interpersonal relationship you share, the more intense your sex life will become.

The greatest sexual pleasure you can achieve comes from understanding your sexual personality and that of your partner, then planning around your mutual needs. An emotional sexual may use self-hypnosis to heighten the sex drive and increase the frequency of relationships. You will also want to plan your foreplay so that you always account for the emotional sexual's naturally slower arousal time.

As I have indicated in this chapter and throughout the book, a greater understanding of one's sexual personality is always the first step to sexual pleasure. Go back to the chapter that fits you and re-read it and enjoy the dramatic changes you will experience.

Index